The Home Place

The Drake family around 1895, the only known photograph of the entire group.

"The Home Place

A Memory and A Celebration"

by Robert Drake

MEMPHIS

MEMPHIS STATE UNIVERSITY PRESS
MEMPHIS, TENNESSEE

ACKNOWLEDGMENTS

"A Christmas Visit," © 1976 by the Christian Century Foundation, is reprinted by permission from the 22 December 1976 issue of *The Christian Century*.

"Daddy the Talker, Daddy the Lover," © 1975 by the Christian Century Foundation, is reprinted by permission from the 6–13 August 1975 issue of *The Christian Century*.

"The Forty-two Game," © 1977 by the Christian Century Foundation, is reprinted by permission from the 28 December 1977 issue of *The Christian Century*.

"Portrait in Black and White," © 1979 by the Christian Century Foundation, is reprinted by permission from the 24 October 1979 issue of *The Christian Century*.

The quotation on page 152 is from "Blue Girls" in *The Selected Poems of John Crowe Ransom*, 3rd ed., rev. and enl., © 1969 by Alfred A. Knopf, Inc., and is reprinted by permission of the publisher.

The following selections appeared originally in *Modern Age:* "The Home Place," "The Grace of God at the Maple Grove Methodist Church" (entitled there "The Grace of God at Maple Grove Methodist"), "Eashel," "Grandma," "The Picture Frame," "King Lear at Maple Grove," and the epilogue, "The Old Tales, the Old Times," and are reprinted here by permission of the publisher.

Most of the old photographs in this book are the work of my uncle, the late Rev. W. L. Drake. The new photographs are by Michael O'Brien.

Manufactured in the United States of America

Library of Congress Cataloging in Publication Data

Drake, Robert, 1930-
   The home place.
   1. Drake, Robert, 1930-   2. Drake family.
3. Family—Tennessee, West.   4. Tennessee, West—
Biography.   I. Title.
F442.3.D7   929'.2'0973   80-24110
ISBN 0-87870-198-2

Contents

This book is dedicated to the memory of
WILLIAM BALL DRAKE
and
ELIZABETH BURKS DRAKE
and their children,
one of whom was my father.

❧ Prologue: The World of the Drakes

THIS IS THE BOOK that I was perhaps born to write though I probably could not have written it until now. It is the story of my father's family, from the time when he and his four brothers and two sisters were young, growing up in rural West Tennessee around the turn of the century, until only one brother of all the family remained alive. It is also the story of my father's parents—of his father, a Virginian and a Confederate veteran, and of his mother, a lifelong resident of West Tennessee. My mother and her family appear on the stage too, but, for the most part, only as they are connected or compared with the Drakes. I also am a character here—the observer, the listener, the recorder, the historian—but I do not want to take the Drakes' story away from them, no matter how much I may have learned about myself in my quest for the truth about them. To discover, to try to come to terms with their past, is also, in some measure, an endeavor to come to terms with myself, an incidental endeavor at first but perhaps an ultimate one in time.

What is it that makes the Drakes worthy of study? Is there anything of interest to the outsider about them or is their significance only genealogical, something to be pondered and studied by only their dutiful descendants? They were, in many ways, an extraordinary family; they were "close," as we say, loving, affectionate among themselves, but also open and welcoming to the outsider. By no means clannish, they were includers rather than excluders: the family, for them, was no tight little corporation in which they could see themselves over and over in one another and love only themselves as reflected in one another. It was, rather, a flexible structure, based on blood and propinquity, to be sure, but always ready and eager to take in as many outsiders as possible to share their happiness.

Theirs was a happiness based on *love*, the word I keep coming back to again and again when I think about the Drakes. It was much in their mouths (they told one another over and over how much they were loved) though it was certainly not vitiated thereby. They were also demonstrative: hugging, kissing, and touching came naturally to them and gave outward and visible manifestation of inner grace and joy. They loved one another and felt loved in return, and it would never have occurred to them not to show it. They also seemed to share love in their talk and in their tales.

Talk is another word which inevitably comes to mind when I think of the Drakes. They were all splendid raconteurs, each with characteristic differences of course but shaped and formed by the fine tradition of talk in the family and by the high standards of talk in the community outside the family. At the root of all this talk, I believe, lay joy, which is what I think they mainly wanted to communicate to others and among themselves—joy that they had been blessed with such fine parents, such fine brothers and sisters, such fine neighbors; it was ultimately, I believe, joy in all God's Creation, which He had made and, we are told, looked on with approval. But there was nothing indiscriminate about this joy. The Drakes knew about evil; they knew about the world. But they believed in God and His providence; they believed in the Good News of the Gospels, and they rejoiced. They were rooted in the goodness of God and the joy of the Lord, and these they shared, passed on, gave life to in their talk and in their love. And the gift which they had been given they in turn passed on to others. This is the central truth about them, I believe.

They always had enough to eat and drink; they had clothes for their backs and a house to live in. But their riches were not the riches of this world; indeed they were often heard to express contempt for those who gave all their time and attention to laying up for themselves treasures on earth. What would have been the good, they would have asked, of enriching the body at the expense of the soul? That was where they seemed to believe the single-minded accumulation of this world's goods led. They were by no means improvident or thriftless, but money as such was not their first priority. They therefore never had much of it and thus were denied many opportunities we would consider essential today. It was a life of quality they had, not quantity, and they never seemed to wish for anything else.

It may have been just as well. My grandfather, their father, was not a man to build an empire or even carve out much of a niche in the wilderness: he belonged to more settled ways, more prosperous times back in Virginia. Times were hard in the rural South seventy or eighty years ago. There was little money anywhere. But what other resources did the Drakes have? They had their God, and they had their family. What else? They had their geography, and they had their history. It was the land which gave them their subsistence, and they had a piety for it, as they seem to have had for all Creation. The idea of exploiting land to the point of depletion and exhaustion would have been inconceivable to them—and this long before ecology became a fashionable cause. After all, were they not here simply as stewards; was not the land itself something to be held in trust and treated with respect, almost reverence? No one ever owned it; he was only lent it for a short time and would presumably some day have to render an account of his stewardship. Beyond the land of course lay the community around them, their neighbors and friends, and beyond that lay the county and so on and on to the limits of the big wide world. But with the latter the Drakes could not be bothered: they did well enough to cope with day-to-day life in their own community. After all, was not the wider world simply their own place multiplied a hundredfold? If they knew their own time and place, would they not inevitably know something of other times and places? Such a view, if followed too strictly, could have led to the narrowest kind of provincialism. But that never seemed to be the case with the Drakes who were all only too willing to concede that different times and different places had equal validity for those who inhabited them. And they could share in such concerns because they knew well their own time and place.

History they had in great supply, for my grandfather, the Confederate veteran, resided in the house and was the living embodiment of the past. For the Drakes, history was something they took for granted but naturally regarded with respect: it would never have occurred to them to condescend to history. On the other hand, they never needed to "discover" history the way that many people in the modern world seem to today in their hankering for nostalgia and their longing for "roots." History, for them, was simply something they had, and it inevitably shaped and defined the individual and his perceptions of the world. Along with geography, it provided the individual with definition, with identity: it was his "skin," which he could never get outside of. Indeed, he would try to do so at his peril. History and geography, then, gave the Drakes their own time and place as well as a healthy respect for all times and all places and their own relation to them. Further, they gave the Drakes their own identities: they knew *who* they were because they knew *where* they were and *when* they were. Thus the Drakes knew early the world's body around them and were at home there, with no alienation from either time or place. And their lives were whole and full.

It had to go, of course. The Drakes died off, the times changed; thus the world has ever been. Yet they live on in my memory and in the hearts of all who knew them as the unique beings that they were. Modern times have arrived in their world. Farms like the one where my father and his brothers grew up are scarcer and scarcer these days: indeed, the whole farming economy has changed. TVA has arrived, as have any number of other modern conveniences like good roads, more efficient automobiles, and all the rest. Increasingly, communities like the Drakes' have been harder pressed to maintain any sense of identity. We live lives of hurry, lives of waste; no longer can we emulate the Drakes' slow-paced world. Yet who can say that their world and its sanctions are any less meaningful to us today? Perhaps they constitute some sort of witness against us, some kind of rebuke to us—we who live lives of such divided aims, such frenetic activity.

The Drakes and their world—whatever else they may have been—were solid, and they were whole. The home meant something; the family meant something; the community meant something. They were all very real entities which nourished and sustained the individual while at the same time providing him with a sense of belonging to something greater than himself: they gave order and meaning to his life. Already present in the Drakes' own times were the seeds of change and disruption, threats to their world in the forms of heartless technology, brutalizing standardization, and "efficiency" at all costs. Also, because they were based on different assumptions about God and man, there loomed menaces which went beyond the Drakes' framework in the form of affections which devoured instead of gave, love which sought only itself to please, and suffering and sorrow. But they were dormant, on the whole, during the Drakes' heyday as a family—that time from 1895 to 1915. Only with the breakup of the family, which began with the death of my grandmother in 1917, and the social and economic changes which followed the first World War did those hostile forces begin to loom large.

This is not to discount the great legacy of the Drakes—what I feel they left me and all their other heirs—as worthless or useless in the modern day. If anything, I treasure it all the more, because it does so often seem to run against the grain of modern times. It is these memories of their doings, so often recounted in their own voices, that I listen to more and more as I grow older. These old "Drake tales," as I have always called them, speak of a life rooted in affections for blood, time, and place and in that which cannot be seen, much less measured. They speak of a life that is whole and not confused and divided in its objects; they give evidence of a sense of belonging, a sense of significance provided by meaningful structure and form. One cannot go home again, of course; the past can never be fully recaptured, we know. But it seems to me still that the Drake past, if not recoverable, is at least ponderable; and I love both it and them for what I feel has been their great gift to me—the legacy of their lives, their times, and, above all, their great love.

The pieces which follow tell something of this history: the Drake family's origins in West Tennessee, their flowering there and subsequent decline. More or less, the order of the pieces in each section constitutes a kind of chronology within the total structure of the Drake experience, the different aspects of which are here revealed. They may therefore be read in sequence, though each piece is itself something of an entity. They often overlap, and, if an analogy from music is in order here, I see them as constituting some sort of song cycle rather than an operatic or symphonic whole. They approach the whole truth, the heart of the matter, now from this side, now from that, emphasizing now this aspect, now that. Yet the whole is greater than the sum of the parts, and the final effect is more cumulative than progressive, I believe. Instead of a single over-arching narrative, many stories are presented here, all of them organic in the complete story of the Drakes. That is what I hope I have written here—the story of a family rather than that of the individuals who composed it, the story of a world that is gone but is by no means dead.

As I intimated earlier, this search for the truth about the Drakes inevitably revealed to me something of the truth about myself: I am their heir in spirit as well as in body. I see in myself the pieties, the loyalties they cherished; but I see as well those tendencies which may work against such allegiances. Thus I am both Drake and anti-Drake. They lived in their time, and I must live in mine. But I think I value more than ever what was real, what was good in them—things I had always taken for granted before, never stopping to weigh and consider—especially now that I have seen, with age, with maturity, what the alternative to such sterling qualities can be.

I am, finally, proud of the Drakes not for what they did (they really did not do very much) but for what they were and still are in the minds and hearts of all those who knew them. They accomplished little as this world rates such things; they accumulated little of this world's goods. Some people would say that they did not amount to much, but I beg to differ. They lived, they loved, they laughed, they wept—and all from the heart as well as the head. Above all, they spent themselves freely, whether in their actions or in their affections. They gave liberally of such means as they had, but they spent prodigally from those gifts of the spirit which were theirs. They not only talked; they acted. And verily they have had their reward. They showed the world then—they still show me today—what the good life can truly be.

Are the pieces which follow then strictly history? No, because I have changed some names, dates, and details of the action to give better shape to the picture of the Drake experience and occasionally

to avoid embarrassment and to protect the innocent, as we say.
Perceptive readers will have little difficulty identifying the county
seat of Woodville as Ripley, Tennessee, the county itself as Lauder-
dale, and the country community where the Drakes grew up as
Hurricane Hill. But whatever facts, mostly small ones, I have invented here are still close to the ultimate truth about the Drakes, I
believe. Certainly, I have not been aiming at that curious phenomenon, the nonfiction novel, of which we have heard much in
these latter years. Rather, I have wanted the Drakes' story to seem
something of a rounded whole though not, finally, at the expense of
essential historical truth. All the liberties I have taken with fact here
have been prompted by that consideration. Occasionally, therefore,
the words may falter, but the song sings true.

The Home Place

For us, the long remembering
Of all our hearts have better known. . . .
— Donald Davidson, "Southward Returning"

1

THE DRAKE PAST

MY GRANDFATHER, William Ball Drake, was born at Ballsville in Powhatan County, Virginia, in 1846. His father died when he was quite young, and his mother took him and his brother and sisters back to live with her father, Isham G. Ball. It was on his plantation that they all grew up. I have heard that my Great-grandfather Ball was related to the same Ball family as George Washington's mother and that he was an *infidel* (a terrible word, both to his contemporaries and to me as a youngster) until late in life, when he was converted through reading a book which set forth the truths of the Christian religion more persuasively than he had ever before seen them. At any rate, the Balls or the Drakes, perhaps both, were *big* Baptists. (One hears of *devout* Catholics, *staunch* Presbyterians, *prominent* Methodists, but always *big* Baptists.) My grandfather, "Pa," as his children and grandchildren all called him, was reared in that faith, in the Mt. Moriah Baptist Church in Ballsville. I have returned there to explore and take pictures, and the church (or more probably its successor) still stands, complete with an old-fashioned country graveyard right outside.

In the cemetery are buried Pa's older brother, Uncle Werter, who for many years was the official physician for Hollins College, and, I think, his sister, Aunt Laura Hurt, and some of her family. But really there are few Drakes there: Pa left Virginia as a young man, and the rest of the family scattered. Though he became a Methodist after he married my grandmother in Tennessee, he continued, as did all his children, to speak of Mt. Moriah as *the* church in their past, part of their history, even though most of them would never see it. The church they were all born into and reared in was the Maple Grove Methodist Church in Tennessee. While that was the church in their daily lives, Mt. Moriah always lay in the background, some point of the past that was peculiarly theirs, that gave a meaning and direction to their lives in the present. And they could not have imagined being without it.

I know very little of my grandfather's story until he ran away from school while still in his teens to fight in the Civil War; he did so as a private in the artillery, a member of Hardaway's Battery in the Army of Northern Virginia. He was at Spottsylvania Courthouse, and I have his parole papers, signed on that Palm Sunday in 1865 at Appomattox, framed and hanging on the wall of my living room today. I know little of how his family fared during the war except that they, like many others, lost "nearly everything they had." Pa then set out with a first cousin on the Ball side of the house for West Tennessee, hoping there to recoup his fortunes, which I am sorry to say he never did. The cousin returned to Virginia after a year, but Pa remained and there met my grandmother, Elizabeth Ann Burks. They were married in January of 1873, and, because there was no Baptist church in that community, Pa joined the Methodist church with my grandmother, who, much to the consternation of the Virginia relatives, was already a Methodist. They never really forgave him for such treachery.

The first of their seven children was born in November of that same year, and in due course they were to have five sons and two daughters. My father was their fifth child and fourth son, and he was born in 1885. Thus I always felt a generation gap in my own existence because I was not born until 1930 when my father was forty-five and my mother was forty. To this day, I am still more at ease with older people than with the young or the middle-aged; I have never needed to "discover" the past. I grew up with history in the house—

my Confederate-veteran grandfather, his five middle-aged sons (the two daughters had long been dead), and always the talk that swirled around me of the war, hard times, the deaths of friends and loved ones, and the old times out at Maple Grove. These were part of my immediate inheritance; indeed, I often felt that I had been born into the past instead of the present.

Such a heritage contrived to set me apart from my contemporaries from the beginning. There was a time when I found it tiresome to live with; I was almost ashamed of it and would have given a great deal to be "modern," with younger parents who had younger ways. I realize now, though, how much the past had to offer me and how much it did give me, things I could not have appreciated at the time but which have become incalculably precious to me now: a sense of history, the sobering *exempla* that reside therein, and always, always a piety for what might be long gone but by no means finished. Past and present were certainly not discrete and discontinuous for me but part of the same fabric, the warp and woof of which would ultimately stretch on into the future. Rather than "living in the past," as we often say, I was thus given some understanding of time itself, an apprehension all too often lacking in the world today.

It took me some time to value this legacy, however. The Drakes all loved to talk on those Sunday afternoons when we went out to visit my grandfather—all about old times in the country, when they were growing up, out at Maple Grove, at the home place. It was tiresome and exasperating for a small boy to have to sit quietly ("children should be seen and not heard") and hear the same old stories told and retold a hundred times over: did they not ever want to live in the modern world, to get away from the country and see the big wide world outside? That was never going to happen to *me*; I made up my mind early about that.

Yet as I grew older, as I grew away from Maple Grove and the home place and all it stood for in the Drakes' lives, I began to understand and perhaps appreciate more what had been done for all of them. It was not just a place; it was a home and a way of life. It was where they all still belonged, though they might have moved out to Woodville, the county seat, only three miles away. It was where they had first known life; it was where they had first known love and,

The Drakes at the home place around 1915.

of course, sorrow. It therefore defined them forever afterwards, no matter where they worked or wandered. I know enough now to value that knowledge, that gift, very much indeed. Many of us in the world today do not seem to be from anywhere; we do not belong anywhere. Existing only in our own insides, many of us are thereby cut off from participation in anything like the totality of life and human experience: we are alike ignorant, even contemptuous, of and perhaps not a little afraid of both history and geography.

The Drakes had all this and more going for them: the past, present, and future as a seamless garment laid out before them and a deep affection for them all but most of all for the past as a definer of the present, a projector of the future, and the one thing they could count on but of course never possess. It was a shared past, uniting them all in the memories, the joys, and the sorrows which belonged to them all. As an only child, I realized I could perhaps never know such feelings except from the outside, but I tried more and more to work my way into the Drake past to see and to learn for myself what its significance was for them, what its significance might be for me who came so long after the event and, to some extent, as one who came alone.

I think I have learned a great deal about the Drakes and their past since I have been grown; I am afraid I really could not have learned it sooner. What was the substance of their life; what was its shadow? What were its prime loyalties, its prime movers? What were my grandfather and grandmother really like, and what part did they play in the lives of their children? What were the children like themselves? How did they, all of them, feel about the family as an entity? What did they have in their lives that could make them loyal to their shared memories so many years later? In the pieces which follow I hope to come to terms with, if not find some answers for, such questions, such considerations, as these.

❧ The Home Place

IF YOU ARE NOT CAREFUL, you will miss the home place when you drive out to Maple Grove. That was the small farm where my father and his four brothers and two sisters had grown up seventy or eighty years ago, and, though they had been gone from there for many years, they continued to call it the home place all their lives. It was as though no matter how far away they moved (and only Uncle John, the oldest, who was a Methodist preacher, ever left the county) they all needed and wanted the home place as the fixed center of their lives. Even though they had been long gone from there, their parents and sisters dead, their home "broken up," as they said, it was as if they could not bear to let go of the idea of home—home at Maple Grove, where they had all grown up, where Pa and Grandma (they all called her "Ma," which I used to think tacky when I was little) gave them the time and the place where they belonged. Oh, yes, they might have moved into Woodville, as Daddy and Uncle Buford had done, or down to Barfield, like Uncle Wesley. But that would never be home for any of them in the sense that the home place had been.

I could never understand it when I was growing up, though. The other brothers had long since sold their interest in the home place to Daddy and Uncle Buford, who were in business together, but they all still called it the home place as if Pa and Grandma and all the rest of them were still alive and living there. It was only about a hundred acres big, had belonged to Grandma, and was about all the inheritance any of them had. Pa, as a transplanted Virginian and the son of slave-owners, never took much to the actual work of farming. He had much rather sit on the porch and talk about old times in Virginia,

8

when he was growing up on the plantation, or the battles he had fought in in the Civil War. I gather my grandmother made the farm pay or at any rate supported the family out of what she was able to save from the cotton money and from the butter and eggs she sold. So they lived and lived pretty well too on the small farm—what we would today call subsistence farming, I suppose.

To them of course the home place was more than just subsistence, just living. It was a whole way of life. From it they ventured up the lane to the main road (dirt then, gravel later, asphalt today), to see their neighbors, to go out to Woodville on Saturday, and always, always to go up to the Maple Grove Methodist Church on Sunday. That was their other home—the church—and in those days it was not only the religious center of the community, but the social and educational center as well. There was a schoolhouse behind the church, but it was only open a few months out of the year: during winter and laying-by time, in July and August, after the crop was made. The church was the real hub of the wheel which was the community, and to it the various families made their way along the different routes (spokes) from their homes. My father's family moved back and forth between the home place and the church in the pattern which defined their lives. The church was the community in its totality, fully in being and realized; the home place was the community in little, perhaps fragmented, reflecting other such small communities (families) but as important, as self-sufficient on its own grounds. The church and the home place were thus not antagonistic or mutually exclusive; rather, they were complements of each other, and neither would have been complete alone.

When I first remember the home place, Pa lived there with a family who farmed the place for him and more or less looked after him, too. Though my grandfather had long been widowed, my grandmother's presence did not seem altogether lacking in the house. I had never known either of my grandmothers, and perhaps I simply wanted to imagine Grandma's influence as still present there: I needed a grandmother badly, I felt. Perhaps, now that I think of it, her presence was felt, but not so much in the tangible objects of the household, the old but modest furniture, the few nineteenth-century "classics" on the book shelves. Rather, she hov-

Dirt road leading to the home place.

ered in and around the conversations when Daddy and the other brothers went out to see Pa, usually on Sunday afternoons; they could not keep from reminding each other of what Ma had said about this or done about that.

A more palpable symbol of the past was the old reed organ in the parlor; it had belonged to their younger sister, who had died tragically—young, beautiful, talented, and much beloved. The organ stood for her in some way nothing in the house did for Grandma. (We had Grandma's dining room table that Daddy said all of them had grown up fighting around at our house, but it did not really represent Grandma to me; it was detached, disembodied from the home place.) But the younger sister's death, only a few months before Grandma's, was still such a great grief to them that, even after many years, they never took much notice of the organ, almost shied away from it, in fact. I was charmed with it, though, and loved to pump away at the pedals and wheeze out a few chords. But Daddy refused to let me have it tuned and brought into town so that I could have fun playing it. He said it belonged out at the home place, and that was that, but of course I did not understand. Now that I think of it, why did he not feel the same way about the dining room table? Perhaps, for him, it represented the vitality and continuity of the home place and what it stood for, perpetuated in our own house, and thus gave order and meaning to the present. But the organ represented only the dead past—sweet, sad, and embalmed in memory but no longer alive in the present. The organ was "over with"; the table was not.

When the Drakes talked about what all had gone on at the home place when they were growing up, who all had visited them, how many had sat down at the dinner table at one time on some important occasion (the children of course waiting for the second table), it was hard to imagine how so much action could have taken place in such a small house (only two bedrooms downstairs and a loft above for the sons). I wondered if perhaps their imaginations were running riot, but apparently they were not. Their house and their purse were small, but their hearts and minds were large, and that was what really mattered.

There were the old photographs, too, to prove it, some made by itinerant photographers, but most by Uncle John when he took up photography on the side. They show the family—all the brothers and the younger sister, along with Grandma and Pa—standing together on the ground in the "L" of the back porch and constituting the group that Uncle John always dearly loved to photograph. (I used to think he did not care who was in the group as long as he could photograph a lot of people all under one roof. He always wanted to include as many people as possible whether they actually belonged or not, Drakes, whoever, or whatever.) And there they stand, ready to explode into life at any minute, only arrested for the brief moment of picture-taking. But one senses their vitality and their affection for each other, the energy, and the action all the same.

There are Pa and Grandma, he leaning against the porch with one hand inside his fastened coat in a grand nineteenth-century conventional pose. He has no tie on, and one suspects he may have been haled in from the field for the occasion. Grandma is looking down at the ground somewhat demurely (she hated having her picture taken, they said), and the younger sister looks aside, and you expect her to blush any moment from sheer innocence and maiden purity. The brothers are a mixed lot: Uncle John, if he is not the photographer, looking majestic and grand in an attitude befitting an incipient preacher (coat and tie for him and standing collar, too); Uncle Wesley looking troubled but with a smile ready to break around his lips; Uncle Jim trying his best to look like the hardworking farmer he became, affecting perhaps the down-home country man a little much, but looking, too, as through he might burst into laughter at any moment; then Daddy posed (merely for a laugh?) with a derby hat on, looking solemnly into space; and finally Uncle Buford, the baby, still in skirts. The photograph swarms with life, with love, and reciprocal feelings for one another of the strongest sort. The viewer feels all that, just as he feels they are all on the verge of laughter, always characteristic of the Drakes. They took their love for one another and for the home place itself too seriously not to see the fun in it all. Love and laughter surely must have gone hand in hand for them judging from the tales they used to tell, loved to tell, on each other and the old times at the home place. They loved the most, could laugh the most, and could therefore grieve the most when the circle was broken, the group picture violated by death and time. (The older sister had died so long ago that she was not in most of the photographs, but she still loomed in their thoughts and conversation.) After her, Grandma and the younger sister were the first to go.

Pa, in his last years and after he broke his hip, moved away from the home place, up to Uncle Jim's on the main road out to Woodville and the church. Today, after all the rest have died, Uncle Buford owns the home place, but I notice he mostly calls it "the farm." (Does he hate to think of the home place as such still when it is no longer a home?) For some years, when he and Daddy owned the home place together, there were tenants living in the house itself. They abused it so that he and Daddy finally had it torn down. Perhaps that was the beginning of calling it "the farm": when the house was torn down, it was no longer the home place. I cannot say for sure. I do know that years later, when Maple Grove was having a Farm Bureau community improvement drive, my cousin Laura, Uncle Jim's daughter, and some others in the community who were heading the effort tried giving names to all the farms in the neighborhood (mostly for show, I thought). She asked Daddy whether he would object to their calling the home place "Wild Locust Farm" because there was one such tree right beside the gate at the turnoff

The home place: the last days. Photo by Michael O'Brien.

from the main road. Daddy said to go ahead, but in his mind it would always be the home place and nothing else.

He did have a joke about its size, though, which, as I have said, was small. One of his friends, Mr. Ed Gaines, owned a lot of land in the north end of the county, and every time we passed his farm, Daddy would proclaim expansively, with a great sweep of his hand, "Now just as far as you can see belongs to Ed Gaines." Because not much of the home place was visible from the main road, Daddy would do the same thing there: "Just as far as you can see belongs to the Drakes." I was always tickled at that and would laugh accordingly.

I think about it still when I drive past the home place, where the lane turns off that used to go to the house. Perhaps Daddy was wiser than he knew; it was a lot they owned, the Drakes. In some ways it was a whole world—as far as you could see both then and now. Who could have been given, or wanted, more than the home place gave them? Few people today are that fortunate. Uncle Buford now has it rented to a cattle man, and perhaps it is another small farm to most people. But I still like to think of it as the home place. And I am very grateful for the wonderful gift it gave the Drakes in their time and what I feel it still gives me today through their lives, through my memories—the living and the dead, past and present, not separate and apart, but, in the end, joined forever in a veritable communion of saints, a whole world of grace and joy and love.

❧ The Grace of God at the Maple Grove Methodist Church

WHY THERE WAS NO Baptist church at Maple Grove I do not know. Baptists certainly thrived in that soil and on that water (particularly, for them, the water!). Perhaps the Methodists had simply gotten there before they did and beaten them out; after all, it was a small community. Pa may even have been typical of the times, which, for all their sectarianism, were fairly tolerant, perhaps even characteristic of the frontier, with its openness and freedom. He may even have helped to set a pattern of behavior because, when he arrived at Maple Grove from Virginia after the Civil War, he was a lifelong, dyed-in-the-wool Baptist. But there was no Baptist church there, as I said, and he married my grandmother, who was a Methodist, and joined the church with her. I suppose that was the last he ever thought of it, but the Virginia kinfolks never forgot it and more or less held it against him until the day he died. Of course, he did not see them often anyhow—mainly when he went back for Confederate reunions. (Virginia was always "back," suggesting its historic primacy, I suppose, while Texas was always "out," which conjured up visions of the tall and uncut.) The Virginia folks all belonged to the Mt. Moriah Baptist Church at Ballsville in Powhatan County, and that was the hub of the universe as far as they were concerned. Sooner or later they were all buried there, too. (It turned out to be Maple Grove for Pa, and Mt. Moriah for them.) I always thought it was more or less six of this and half a dozen of the other: people have to build their lives around something, I suppose. But I doubt that some of them, particularly the Virginia Baptists, would have seen it that way.

Daddy and his brothers were all brought up in the bosom of the

15

Maple Grove Methodist Church, and that was all they knew or cared to know until much later in life when they were grown and married and had moved into town from the country. In some ways they never got away from Maple Grove and the Maple Grove Methodist Church because they all talked about it for the rest of their lives. For one thing, they all seemed to have had so much fun there. I know years later when one of the aunts (the widow of one of my uncles) was talking to me about it, she said, "O, they did have a lot of fun at the church back then. But it's all different now. Why, they're so dignified up there, I don't suppose anyone dares crack a smile." Now I myself do not think the community, or the world, has gotten any more sober-sided or serious-minded since the Drakes resided at Maple Grove; it is simply that they have other outlets for humor now, other places to play. The church has become another building with a specific function and use for them; it is not the hub of their universe anymore. What is? The television screen? The football field? Perhaps no single thing, no single place does, or can, now fulfill the function for anybody that the Maple Grove Methodist Church did for all the Drakes in the old days. In some ways I think that is a loss: the church is now no longer the everyday center of community life but another slot to plug into one day a week; it serves one purpose and one purpose only. While it all sounds very correct and very proper, the new role is also, I think, very dull and very dead. Where is the old life? Where is the old fun now?

They did have fun in the old days, but religion was not any the less meaningful to them for all that. The Christian gospel is, after all, a fairly ridiculous proposition. (God loves man, it says, not because he is good—which he is not—or clean or anything else he may be or may have done himself, but simply because He wants to and it is His good pleasure. And that does seem like a damned fool thing for Him to do. The grace of God may be the Good News we have all been waiting for, but it is something of an absurdity too.) I do not think the Drakes saw anything inconsistent between religion and fun though of course they probably would not have said so in so many words. The world to them, for all its faults, was good (after all, God had made it Himself), and life was good though hard and demanding in the work and the sweat required on the farm. It was good to be alive.

Surely, the joy of the Lord and the delights of this world had something in common.

When I was little, I used to get tired of all the stories about the Maple Grove Methodist Church. For one thing, the Drakes told them all over and over again whenever they got together. It all used to bore me and I wondered why it did not affect them the same way. Who in the world wanted to hear all those old stories that everybody already knew by heart anyway? Well, of course, years later, after most of them were dead, I realized that they had not been telling all those stories because they were new, but simply because they were good: novelty might wear off but quality never did. But that is something you cannot know until you are grown. When they told and retold those stories, the past was re-created for them, full of life and meaning; it continued to give meaning to their lives into the present. Not a mere sentimental exercise in nostalgia, theirs was an act of piety which continually renewed and refreshed by reminding them of their original and abiding roots in their time and place, of their reality, which included both past and present and looked forward into a future which was discerned through a past recalled and a present lived in the light of this recollection—sobering, bless-

Interior of the Maple Grove Methodist church.

ing, humbling, rewarding. Past, present, and future—all were part of an overarching eternity which, again, you cannot know until you are older, especially in the world in which we live today, where often the past is either ignored or exploited and the present and future are seen as the only realities.

Anyhow, the Drakes had fun at church, and, as I said earlier, not because they were not reverent: God and fun were not mutually exclusive but perhaps complementary. Many of their favorite stories had to do with the preachers who served that church and their various eccentricities and peculiarities. One of them, a man new on the circuit, told them after his first sermon there that he could have killed hogs and hung the meat up right there in church with no fear of its spoiling because they were the coldest bunch of people he had ever preached to in his life. Now I do not think he was a fire-eating evangelist who wanted to see an excessive display of emotion, but he did want to touch their hearts (remember Wesley sitting in Aldersgate Church and feeling his heart strangely warmed?). It was not a cold congregation at all, Daddy said; they were all on their good behavior for his first sermon. Certainly, they could let themselves go enough at the right time, as in the middle of a protracted meeting when Cousin Birdie Sneed would start roaming the aisles for souls to wrestle with and bring to Christ. Because she had a harelip and always insisted on kissing her converts, all the young folks who had not joined the church would start jumping out of windows and doors when they saw her coming.

Sometimes young people did not jump soon enough, however: young Tom Maynard had been carrying on a prolonged courtship with Mary Ann Graves, and everybody thought it was high time they got married. But Tom did not make a move in that direction until old man Graves, Mary Ann's father—who had been a steward in the church since before Christ, Daddy said—prayed over Tom when the young man went to the altar in answer to the preacher's calling for mourners to come forward. Mr. Graves laid his hands on young Tom's head and said, for all the world to hear, "O, Lord, soften this young sinner's hard heart because, as sure as God made little apples, he's going to marry my daughter." Young Tom might not have been thinking of marriage before that, but he knew he had

better do so then. He and Mary Ann were married right after the
revival was over.

When mourners' benches started becoming a thing of the pas
Daddy said it was a bad thing. He said, "You quit preaching Chr
crucified and take the mourners' benches out of the churches,
you might as well close the doors." Although Daddy was not incl
to shout in church himself, he also thought the elimination of
means of expression might be a loss. "Why," he said, "if you st
shouting in church now, they'd probably have you arrest
disturbing the peace." I am not sure that he ever thought r
was necessarily peaceful ("not peace by a sword"?). As he
needed to have some "spizerinctum" in it. (What would v
now—charisma?) Anyhow, it had certainly not been lik
Maple Grove in the old days. When the preacher called
during a big meeting, all but the most hardened would g
altar to get "reconditioned," as Daddy put it. (Meth
supposed to be great believers in back-sliding and falling
unlike the Baptists who believed "once in grace, alway
Sometimes the preacher would call on various repent
offer individual prayers. There were memorable m
once old Mr. Jenkins ran out of something to pra
middle of his supplication and just said, "O, Lord, b
stop to rest," which was followed by dead silenc
Drakes, all of whom were having a giggling spell.
Drake volunteered to pray when the preacher as
to lead the repentant in prayer. Afterwards, on
neighbor, Mr. James K. Polk Harrison, said to
think it's fine for a man to pray in public. And if t
you do it. But, Bill, don't ever volunteer anym
would die laughing at that story; although Pa
conversation, that was about the only place l
As a transplanted Virginia gentleman, he wa
doing where work was concerned either; the
to death if it had not been for Grandma,

Another time, Uncle Buford, the youn
was naturally shy and retiring, was mor
called for volunteers to pray and one of t

and said, in a stage whisper, "Say one, Buford, say one." Uncle Buford croaked out, "Stir us up, O Lord, stir us up," and then clammed up, turning crimson at his own boldness. They never let him forget that either, and for years afterward, whenever they wanted to put the quietus on him, especially out in public, they would say, "Say one, Buford, say one," and that would be the end of him. They all loved to tell about the time when Daddy was four years old and had learned a verse for Children's Day that went: "Do your best, your very best, and do it all the time." However, when Daddy rose up to recite, scared pop-eyed of course, he said, "Do your best, your very best, and do it in the daytime."

Levity certainly had its place out there. Once Brother Martin, a much loved preacher on the "charge" (as Methodist Churches were often called in those days), walked in to preach a Sunday night sermon. It had been a long day in the hot summertime, and all the young folks were tired and worn out from going to Sunday school and church in the morning and visiting back and forth with each other in the afternoon. When Brother Martin asked, "Young people, what shall I preach about tonight?" Daddy replied, "About twenty minutes." Of course that almost broke up the meeting right there.

Then there were the strange and arresting texts that the various preachers chose for their sermons. One of the most memorable was "Ephraim is a cake not turned." I always thought it was ridiculous, surely invented by one of the Drakes for a laugh, until years later when I was a graduate student at Yale and heard one of the Divinity School professors preach on that very same text (Hosea 7:8). He expounded it as a comment on people's lives without God: they were cakes that had not been turned, in other words, half-baked. (Whoever would have thought Maple Grove would be vindicated in New Haven, Connecticut? I guess, however, stranger things than that have happened in my life.) Then there was the text, "She did and she didn't," which I still believe apocryphal; at any rate, I have never been able to locate it. But there was, for real, the text, "She hath done what she could" (Mark 14:8). It seemed to cover a multitude of things (for example, those of the woman who anointed the Savior's head with oil) and to pretty well nail down the human condition or,

at any rate, man's efforts to ameliorate it, which did not amount to much more than being nice tries. It all looked forward to the grace of God, realizing that no man could succeed alone.

In a curious way I think that is what all the Maple Grove Methodist Church tales—the Drake tales, I called them—added up to: the grace of God and its wonder, its absurdity, and its absolute necessity for poor, foolish, deluded man. What could be funnier, what could be sadder, than man's predicament in this middle state—the glory, jest, and riddle of the world, poor forked creature that he was, with all his strutting and fretting for one brief hour? One was often torn between tears and laughter at the spectacle (were they not simply different sides of the same coin?). The Drakes and their kind chose to laugh, but, at the same time, they knew how to cry, also; all of them were big-hearted, "feeling" creatures to whom both tears and laughter came easily. But what about laughter in church? Given the human animal and his characteristic foolishness, why not? Would God not laugh to see the creature He had so fearfully and wonderfully made always trying to forget his Maker and set up shop on his own, quite literally making a damned fool of himself? How funny, how sad, and yet how human! Surely, that is the long view God must have taken (and He did go in for long views, I supposed). Finally, I think that is the view the Drakes took as well. However, as I said earlier, that is something they could not have put into words then and something I certainly could not have known until I was a lot older myself.

❧ *"You Can Wink, and You Can Blink..."*

THE FIRST TIME Aunt Estelle ever saw my Uncle John, she was staying at the home place, visiting his sister Adeline, the one that everybody called Eashel. Setting out for Haley's Campground, where a big revival was in progress, they traveled in a buggy from the home place to the main road; when they got there Uncle John was sitting on the fence as though he had dropped, completely unexpected, from the clouds or somewhere else out of the blue. To tell the truth, he was unexpected; he had gone off to school out in Texas some months before and had arrived that morning in Woodville on the train without telling a soul in the world he was coming. That was understandable perhaps because the truth was that Uncle John had gotten homesick, pure and simple, and decided to come on back home; I suppose he thought he had better not write the family or they would try to dissuade him. He was already a grown man—and then some (thirty or thereabouts)—and everyone would have thought he was being childish. Although he was the oldest of all the Drake children, he remained something of an innocent all his life. He said that he was nearly grown before he found out about Santa Claus and that then they practically had to catch him and take him out behind the house to tell him. (Mamma said she would have been ashamed to tell that on herself, but then she was probably born knowing about Santa Claus.)

I do not think Uncle John had then thought of going into the ministry, but he was already headed in that direction by temperament. The school in Texas (at Tyler, I think) had a strong Methodist orientation. Because Uncle John had not yet chosen a profession for himself, I suppose the family was concerned about him; he obviously was not cut out to be a farmer, so what else could he do? Perhaps he could have taught school (all the other professions, besides the ministry of course, simply required more money for their preparation than the Drakes could afford).

Some years before—around the turn of the century—Uncle John and Uncle Wesley had begun to dabble in photography. They did their own developing and printing and fixed a darkroom in the woodshed. Uncle John must have been one of the first real photographers in that part of the world, and for the rest of his life photography was almost a second profession for him—always, of course, after the ministry. (I do not think Uncle Wesley stayed with it very long, and anyway he soon went off to work in Barfield.) The Drake family seemed to view Uncle John's photography with a somewhat jaundiced eye: for one thing it was an expensive hobby, and too, they could not believe that anyone could seriously think about it as a business. Uncle John, however, was thoroughly professional about his hobby, and he treated it like a real calling, not just a sideline. Of course he never could hope to make a living out of it in that place in those days; but he did love, as he always said, "getting things down for the record," whether it was a family reunion, a wedding party, or flowers on a grave after the funeral. Today Uncle John's old photographs, which are really professional in quality, help me visualize the times, people, and places—many that I never knew—so important to the Drakes.

Anyhow, the first time Aunt Estelle saw Uncle John he was perched on the fence, a completely unexpected sight. Of course Eashel had a fit because she was so glad to see him, and I think the rest of the family were, too. Naturally they all wanted to know what he was doing home, but, mainly because he was ashamed to tell them he had simply gotten homesick, he said he had been exposed to yellow fever out in Texas. That really frightened Aunt Estelle because she had not been around the Drakes enough yet to know how much they loved to joke and tease. She said she did not draw an easy breath after Uncle John got into the buggy with them, and the whole time they were at the revival she kept looking around for somebody besides the Drakes to take her home.

She must not have had much luck, however, because she did ride

home with the Drakes, and, somewhere along the line, she and
Uncle John began to notice each other. One thing led to another,
and after several years they decided to marry. That was after Uncle
John had definitely decided to enter the ministry, had studied for a
year at Vanderbilt Divinity School, and was holding his first
"charge" on a circuit. I do not know whether Uncle John ever
experienced a personal calling to enter the church; certainly
Methodism in those days placed a lot of emphasis on a personal
experience of conversion and vocation. I think perhaps it never had
occurred to Uncle John, or to any of the other Drakes, to doubt the
role of the church (and God) in their lives; therefore, for Uncle John
to enter the church must have seemed not only suitable but inevit-
able, given his particular character and frame of mind. (Years later
the text for Uncle John's funeral sermon was "Take authority to
preach the gospel." I thought that altogether fitting because he had
given his life to the ministry.) Despite the joking and the fun or
maybe even because of them, he was always serious where matters
of faith and morals were concerned, and none of the Drakes revered
the natural pieties—home, blood, and family—more than he.
(Perhaps his attempts with the camera represented an act of piety,
an effort to hold on to whatever was good in his time and place, to fix
them forever in time "for the record.") Only he of all the children
called his parents by names other than "Ma" and "Pa": he said
"Mammy" and "Daddy," names at once more informal and more
intimate, names which one might have heard used freely by the
Southern Negroes of the day but which ultimately might have been
traced to ancient and hallowed usage in Scotland.

Daddy always said Aunt Estelle had been born with a silver spoon
in her mouth (a figure of speech that I found very disturbing before I
understood what it meant). For one thing, she was a Fisher from out
at Fisher's Crossing. Her father owned so much land that he was
called a planter rather than a farmer though Daddy said the difference was a matter of degree rather than kind. The fact that Mr.
Fisher did not own as much land as he once had showed something
proven by history, according to Daddy: one set of feet goes up the
steps while another set comes down all the time. Aunt Estelle's
older sister, Miss Pearl, had married Mr. Jim Rucker who had made

a lot of money in the furniture business in Alabama. And Aunt Estelle had always been "used to things," as people said, but that did not keep her from falling head over heels in love with Uncle John, who was nearly 16 years older than she, and, because he was going into the ministry, not destined to be a terribly great provider. They were married out at the Fisher's Crossing Methodist Church, and Miss Pearl played the piano for the ceremony. Aunt Estelle was dressed in white satin and wore real orange blossoms in her hair that one of her cousins had sent all the way from Florida. (The newspaper account of the wedding was appropriately detailed and lavish after the manner of those times—1908. Uncle John, who was a "fine manly ornament to the Methodist ministry," was described as wearing "the conventional black.")

Of course, the Drakes made themselves known right from the start. When, after the wedding itself, old Brother Newman, who had performed the ceremony and was something of an old priss, got to bowing and scraping so much over the wedding party and all the stylish guests that he fell right off the church porch, all the Drakes laughed. That was a good initiation for Aunt Estelle into the world of the Drakes right there. They did not have the perverted sense of humor some of their acquaintances, especially in-laws, thought, but they always seemed on the side of sense and reason and consequently enjoyed seeing affectation and pomposity revealed for what they were and thereby deflated. (Of course, Uncle John always said nothing was funnier in the world than seeing a man having a tooth pulled; in later years he was never without a false face around the house to scare his children with, especially around Christmastime when he would put on a Santa Claus mask to sober them up when they got too full of themselves.)

Uncle John and Aunt Estelle went to Memphis for a few days on a wedding trip and when they returned visited the Drakes' home place to pay their respects to Uncle John's family. Miss Pearl, who was a stickler for all the proprieties, had told Aunt Estelle that when they arrived she would have to kiss all her new in-laws. That might have been fine in some families, but the Drakes were always ready to giggle when anybody came down so heavily on the side of custom and ritual that the whole thing was as unnatural and as stifling as a straitjacket. (Not that they discounted genuine family affection; no one could have valued it more.) They were not used to seeing somebody systematically work her way through the whole family, as Aunt Estelle proceeded to do, kissing each one in turn. Most of them submitted with good grace, but Uncle Buford, then barely sixteen, began to feel powerfully uneasy as he saw her approaching him. He was old enough to feel embarrassed about being kissed by an older woman, and for two cents he would have turned tail and run out the back door. Daddy, who was the brother next to him in age and could tell how the wind was blowing, put a restraining hand on Uncle Buford's shoulder and, in a whisper loud enough for everybody to hear, said, "You can wink, and you can blink, but I'm staying with you, Scroggins." The whole family, with the exception of Uncle Buford and Aunt Estelle, burst into laughter then because Daddy's whispered remark brought up one of the oldest, most favorite jokes in the Drake family: when Uncle Buford was a little boy, Brother Scroggins, the preacher, was a dinner guest one Sunday after church. Grandma was running low on her celebrated watermelon rind pickle, which Uncle Buford simply adored, and every time the pickle dish passed him at the table, he would take another piece despite all the significant glances (winks and blinks of the eye) he was getting from the rest of the family. I wonder why no one ever looked at him and said "FHB" ("Family Hold Back"). Maybe he was too young to know what that meant. Finally, Uncle Buford could not stand the situation any longer and, wanting to make his position in the matter thoroughly clear, said "You can wink, and you can blink, but I'm staying with you, Scroggins." Of course, all the Drakes burst into laughter, and, although I never heard how Brother Scroggins reacted, I think everyone thought the incident was a good joke on them rather than him. Too, for what it is worth, I doubt that Uncle Buford ever got a spanking for his impudence.

Anyhow, that was why it was especially funny for Daddy to say what he did to Uncle Buford when Aunt Estelle proceeded to kiss the whole family, and I suppose it was an even better initiation for Aunt Estelle into the world of the Drakes than she had already had. In the years to come, nobody enjoyed telling that tale as much as she, and she would always add, "That was of course before I knew the Drakes very well and understood how much they loved a good joke." This was certainly true, even when the joke was on one of them: that kind they seemed to love best of all. It was as though their laughter was the other side of the coin from their seriousness, their tears. No one felt more deeply for sorrows, those of others as well as their own, and no one shed tears more freely than they, for the world's misery as much as for what was personal and peculiar to them. But they never forgot their priorities: if man was a pitiable creature, he was also at times a ridiculous one—a fact that he had better not forget. All the Drakes' laughter, it always seemed to me, came from some such conviction as this. It was not morbid; it was not perverse. Rather it was quite often purgative and therapeutic, not only for the victims of their jokes, but also for themselves. After I had known them awhile, I concluded finally that there was something loving, something indeed almost of the divine about their laughter, a true gift from God. It is the memory of that gift now that I treasure almost as much as anything else about the Drakes after all these years.

❧ Eashel

SHE WAS THE YOUNGER of my father's two sisters, both of whom died before I was born. The older one was Laura—a name much beloved in my father's family because of the older members who had borne it; and she died in childbirth around the turn of the century, not long ago enough to have become history and therefore meaningful as part of a corporate entity yet not recently enough for me to feel she had impinged in any immediate and personal way on my own life. But Eashel had died thirteen years before I was born, and she was thus close enough to me in time for me to feel that she had existed as a person, that she had been real, and that I could get a fairly accurate idea of her as a living entity across the intervening years.

One thing that fascinated me about her was simply the fact that she was my aunt in her own right (did I compare her to a queen regnant in that respect?), and not merely the wife of one of my uncles. I had plenty of those, and I loved them dearly, but my mother had had no sisters and my father had had only the two, who were dead. Thus all my life I have felt the lack of a "blood" aunt.

Eashel's real name was Sarah Adeline, but she was so tiny when she was born that her brothers said she looked like a little weasel. Of course they could not talk plainly, and it came out sounding like "Eashel," which is the way I have spelled it here. (How they—and she—spelled it, I do not know.) The Drakes were all great on nicknames anyhow: Uncle John was called "Bubber"; Uncle Wesley, who was the next in age after Uncle John, was called "Little Bubber"; Uncle Jim, who still lived at Maple Grove, was called "Teet," a version, I understood, of "Sweet"; and my own father was called "Jucks," of which nobody seemed to know the origin. (Daddy said they must have been trying to say "Sugar" and failed, but I never believed that version.) Uncle Buford was unique in that he apparently had no nickname, but I found out years later that Pa Drake had often called him "Didlum," something he probably would not thank me for setting down here.

For some reason, rightly or wrongly, I always fancied that Uncle Buford was less a part of the Drake family than the others. He had managed to finish high school in Woodville (Daddy was already established in business by then), had gone to Memphis to take a bookkeeping course, and finally had returned to Woodville to go into business with Daddy. This was after World War I, when Uncle Buford had been in the Navy and was stationed at Newport, Rhode Island, and Norfolk, Virginia, from where he was able to visit some of our kinfolks. Uncle Buford had traveled; he had been around to see the big wide world outside of Maple Grove and Woodville; in some ways, he seemed to have broken away, gotten outside the Drake circle. I always imagined that his love, his affection for them, was therefore tempered and qualified by his experience in the outside world. I never felt that the family was as central for him as it was for the others.

On the other hand, I never felt the Drakes were loving themselves to the exclusion of all else: they were clannish but not exclusive. *Family* as a concept was all-important to them, but they never denied that other people's families might be equally important to them: the Drakes would have conceded immediately that they had no particular monopoly on family affection. They certainly were capable, again and again, of loving outside the family. Yes, their first allegiance was unmistakably there, but it was as though the family was, for all its supreme importance, a kind of training ground for other loves and loyalties. Warm, generous, openhanded and openhearted, they loved on beyond the family, the neighborhood, the region to the wide world itself: they loved each other, their friends and relatives, but they also loved General Lee, President Roosevelt, and Winston Churchill.

Where does Eashel fit into all of this? (Hardly anyone ever called her Adeline; therefore I always thought of her as Eashel, and Eashel she will remain.) For one thing, they had all adored her; she had been not only beautiful but also very good. After her death she became a center for all family feeling, an ideal realized briefly but all too soon blighted—the embodiment of love and warmth and beauty, all those qualities they treasured. In some curious way she became a focus for their affection for each other, for the family, and for what they wanted to believe about themselves, even from beyond the grave. I suppose every family, certainly in the South where family as a concept has always been important, has had some flower of the forest cut down in its prime, some last and loveliest that perished before the wintry blasts of the rough world, some lost jewel that can always be looked back to as a continual rebuke to the present and all its endeavors to realize grace and beauty in the here and now. This is the unimpeachable sanction of "what Papa said," "back when things were normal," "if only you had known your grandmother," and "you should have seen the garden last year." These unqualified touchstones abide, out of the past, to take on supreme and infuriating authority in the present, never to be equaled, let alone excelled. They become a kind of Grecian Urn, a kind of nightingale's song, all the more authoritative for being safely unapproachable, cold, and dead.

With first cousins, the author (left) poses at a Drake family gathering around 1938.

This was the way I used to feel about Eashel. Who ever could have been so beautiful, so loving, so beloved? Had not death paradoxically enhanced rather than diminished her stature? She was beautiful, she was good, and she died young—the substance of melodrama all right. What more could one ask? Even now older men and women, mostly in their seventies and eighties, tell me how beautiful she was, how well she played, how well she sang, and always how much they loved her. Was she then always to be preserved in memory without spot or wrinkle, as pure, serene, ineluctable? The past and mortality had won over her, yes, as it does and will do over us all; but had she not, in some sense, triumphed over them? It was wonderful yet perhaps also maddening: no one could ever have been so perfect. Perhaps, I thought, she had been blessed—lucky, if you want to call it that—in her life and equally so in her death. Time would never do so well by me, I felt.

I did not think that the Drakes were consciously creating a myth around Eashel; they simply saw her as beautiful, good, and dead in her youth, and human nature did all the rest. Do we need such myths? Must we have them at all costs? There seems a good deal of evidence to indicate that we do. We crave meaning amidst the random chaos of everyday existence, and myths unquestionably provide meaning. Perhaps, then, it was the myth of Eashel that I resented: she hovered over every family conversation and was an absent guest at every family dinner; she was the nonpareil before whom all others faded and vanished. I do not think the Drakes intended for her to be so (they were clannish but not exclusive, remember), but I was again outside the experience; I had not known her. I had to take the myth at face value, uncorrected, unqualified by experience, and I suppose that was what I resented: not being there to see and decide for myself.

What were the facts of Eashel's life behind the myth? She had grown up with the five brothers (the older sister was already dead), the apple of their and her parents' eyes. She had early displayed a talent for music, both singing and playing, and when she was old enough my father paid for her music lessons. He also bought her clothes after she was grown and was enormously proud of her beauty and talent. She was apparently a devout Christian, and a good part of her life revolved around the Maple Grove Methodist Church. Eventually, she became the organist for the church and even played for the camp meetings at Haley's Campground. There she fell under the influence of an evangelist who preached what was called "the second blessing," which apparently meant a personal consciousness of the descent and continual indwelling of the Holy Spirit within the the individual soul. I suppose this doctrine was a natural enough outgrowth of classic Methodism, with its emphasis on a "personal" Savior and a "personal" conviction of sin and experience of salvation. At any rate, Eashel professed to have received the second blessing, and her reputation for piety and good works grew.

Her life at home, after most of the brothers had grown up and left (she was between Daddy and Uncle Buford in age), seems to have proceeded quietly enough; it was filled with domestic chores and religious duties, for the most part. I gleaned a lot of this information from the diary she kept for several years after she was grown. It is an interesting little book, now in the hands of my cousin who is the oldest of all the Drake grandchildren and the only one of us really to have known Eashel. A note inside the cover indicates that the diary was presented to her by two of the cousins in Richmond when she accompanied my grandfather there for the Confederate reunion in 1910. One of those cousins was later to marry Uncle Jim and thus make us doubly kin. That was yet come and, at the time, Eashel recorded in her diary the excitement of Uncle Jim's going to Richmond for the wedding. The little note of presentation says simply that the diary was being given as a remembrance of her visit to "the Old Dominion." Facts were what I always craved about Eashel. I felt always that she was surrounded by too many layers of myth, perhaps even too many layers of love. Facts would surely puncture the myth or at least deflate it, but unfortunately, the diary conceals as much as it reveals.

On first inspection, her principal concerns there seem to be religion, music, and ironing. She condemns some of her neighbors for going into Woodville for "the show." (Could that have been possibly something as harmless as the old-fashioned, respectable Chautauqua, or could it have been some more worldly diversion like a traveling stock company?) She wishes her community would lead a more godly and serious life, then refers to her practicing—voice and piano both, I take it—and her music lessons. Always, always she is ironing. With a father at home and five brothers in and out all the time (some as yet not married), there must have been plenty of shirts to keep her busy. However, she never mentions washing; my grandmother must have done that. (Years later, when my mother and father were first married, he strictly forbade her to put up a clothesline in the backyard; he said if it had not been for that and the washtub his mother would have been alive that very day.)

Eashel's diary entries continue, quiet and sober, though not dour, for several years (about four or five before her death) and then abruptly cease. Why did she quit keeping it? I will never know. Did she grow weary of the daily discipline involved, lose interest, or what? The most exciting things recorded are her visits to her brothers who were married and settled in Woodville or elsewhere. Once she went to visit Uncle John on his circuit over in the next county. Her entry then reflects how dear and sweet their daughter, my cousin Mary Virginia, was. She was the first grandchild, and I am the last. Mary Virginia now has the diary, carefully protected in plastic. She adored Eashel, too, and still recalls going home to our grandparents' house on a visit and finding Eashel sick in bed. She promptly crawled in bed beside her and had to be forcibly removed.

The diary is more domestic than personal; one gets only a glimmer from the fading pages of what she must have been like. I do know that several years later she met, while on a visit to Uncle John and Aunt Estelle, a young man who was a schoolteacher named Mr. Hunter; he apparently was as diligent and pious as she was. They fell in love and apparently planned to be married. Aunt Estelle, a big talker who Daddy said did not always have her facts straight, insisted that Eashel bought an artificial diamond ring to wear as a "pretend" engagement ring. Daddy said he did not remember anything about that, but I always hoped it was true because it made Eashel sound as though she might have been fun when most of the stories about her always sounded either pious or sad. (Myths, if they are to be comfortable, need some saving humor.) Aunt Estelle, who was exactly Eashel's age, always insisted that she was great fun, but Daddy and the others seemed to prefer their own more sober view as though Eashel's fun would have constituted some sort of profanation of their idealistic image of her.

Not long after her engagement, Eashel became ill (first with a goiter, then typhoid fever) and died. (She had made them promise not to tell Mr. Hunter that she was ill; he therefore did not know of it until too late, and he never forgave them for not telling him because he seems to have loved her so much. He never answered any of Uncle John's letters afterwards.) Her death came in the hot summertime of 1917—that sinister year of our entry into the war, with its dreadful winter to follow, which was to see so many deaths from "flu" and pneumonia.

Both my mother's parents died then (within six weeks of each other) and many other relatives and friends, finally Grandma Drake herself, who they all said simply grieved herself to death about Eashel. Though some of the dearest Virginia kinfolks happened to be with them at the time and all their friends and neighbors gathered around to give aid and support, it was a time the Drakes could hardly ever speak of afterwards without tears. Their home was "broken up" (a dreadful phrase and a very final one, I thought); Pa Drake and Uncle Buford went to live with Uncle Jim and Aunt Mary and then Uncle Buford joined the Navy. No grief had seemed greater for any of them, I gathered, than losing Eashel and Grandma so close together. One of my aunts still remembers that Eashel's music teacher, Miss Bessie Halliburton, sang "His Eye Is on the Sparrow" (Eashel's favorite hymn) at her funeral and that the text for Grandma's funeral sermon was "There remaineth therefore a rest to the people of God" (Hebrews 4:9).

A terrible time, it was for the Drakes not without its blessings, it seems. At the back of Eashel's diary, Uncle John, years later, on the anniversaries of both Eashel's and Grandma's deaths, had made several entries, mostly to the effect that he and Daddy and Uncle Buford—down at Drake Brothers store—had been talking about their beloved dead once again and that they had all agreed that there never had been such a sister and such a mother and about how blessed they had been and how thankful they still were to have had

Eashel standing behind Grandma Drake in an old family photograph.

them in their lives. There was no sorrow then, only thanksgiving for what had been given, was still being given in such memories, in such love.

I could not help being moved by such genuine piety: it is rare enough in the world today. Furthermore, there was no repining there, only thankfulness and praise, which are rare enough at any time. Still I feel that Eashel continues to elude me and always will. I see her photographs (and she was pretty, with a sweet and loving smile); I hear the surviving Drakes talk of her; and I remember what Daddy and the others who are also gone said about her. Yet I can never know her except in the past, in history, which is essentially unknowable. But is it any more so, finally, than the present, for which there are as many views as there are viewers? We keep trying, hoping to approach more nearly the full truth of past and present yet knowing that all the while such complete and final knowledge will ever escape us. So I shall never know Eashel any more than Daddy and his brothers really did. They stood closer to her, that is all.

What was she really like behind the myth? Who can say? And are there not myths or at least masks for all the living as well? Behind the memories, the diary entries, the photographs—behind them all she stands real and palpable, yet remote and enigmatic. I have heard of her all my life; I have searched for her all my life. If I have not found her here, it is because I cannot find even myself here, so little is it given to mortals really to find and to know here and now. But the search itself, behind all the dreams, all the memories, all the voices, is not only an act of piety and love; it is much, much more than that. An obligation and a duty, surely, it is also its own reward in the quiet wisdom, the saving truth, however partial and limited, that it brings—of ourselves and those we love, of our world and their world, which, for all their separateness, are one and indivisible, past and present, now and forever more.

❦ The High–Stepper

MAPLE GROVE, when the Drakes were all growing up out there, seventy or eighty years ago, was a quiet rural community with very little to offer in the way of excitement or entertainment except what you made for yourself at home. Of course, both the religious and social life of the community revolved to some extent around the Maple Grove Methodist Church, which was the scene of regular church services (the second Sunday in the month at night, the fourth Sunday in the morning, and Sunday school every Sunday—all because the church was on the Woodville circuit and the preacher had to be shared with four other communities). It was also the place for meetings of the Missionary Society, gatherings of the Barlow County Singing Convention, and of course for the occasional church social. There the entertainment often took the form of comic skits (once Pa Drake even played the teacher of the "Bodunk School," with lots of unruly scholars, the ringleader of whom was Aunt Mary, Uncle Jim's wife, who was so quiet and sedate when I knew her in later life that I found it hard to imagine her in that role). Mock trials, sometimes called "Green Courts," were also held for all sorts of fanciful misdemeanors.

Folklorists, I imagine, might find in this fertile fields for investigation and turn out learned treatises on the survival of old English and Scottish folkways transplanted in the New World. Such matters have never interested me, however, as much as the people involved in them—how they reacted to the community stress and strain, the community presence, their relationships with their families and friends, and how they behaved as individuals, more or less shaped and formed by tradition and by the community but still very much

37

their own men and women. Actually nothing still is as fascinating—
infuriating, engrossing, or whatever—as folks. They are unpredict-
able and full of surprises of course; but the human "animule," to my
way of thinking, is still pretty much the hairy ape he started out as,
despite the improvements wrought by the civilizing and deodoriz-
ing work of modern science and technology, or even of evolution
itself. The church of course has always called this phenomenon the
"Old Adam" or "Original Sin;" whatever its name, it still exists.
Anyone who doubts it, should just read the newspaper, listen to the
radio or, better still, look in the mirror.

Mr. Bennet in *Pride and Prejudice* asks his daughter Elizabeth at
one point why else we live except to make sport for our neighbors
and then laugh at them in our turn. I suppose this was the attitude of
Maple Grove's dwellers as well—never meaning unkindness or
malice, only interest in what their friends and relations were up
to—they were always up to something, and that meant news and
gossip, but, above all, it meant life.

It was therefore no wonder that residents of Maple Grove sat up
and took notice when they got a new teacher at the schoolhouse
(always pronounced "schoolouse," which confused me when I was
growing up because it suggested some sort of vermin, I thought); the
one-room structure was set back in a grove of trees behind the
church and was in session mostly in the winter, when there was
nothing to do on the farm, and late in the summer, when the cotton
was all laid by. The teacher was a maiden lady with dyed red hair and
only one arm (she had lost the other one to a circular saw at her
father's lumber mill when she was a girl) named Miss Cora Jordan
(pronounced of course "Jurdan"). She had made quite a reputation
for herself over in the next county when the school board there sent
her to teach in a country school where the students were so mean
and ornery that they literally ran off everybody who tried to teach
them. (Their parents were not much better either; they would be
walking along the road by the schoolhouse when school was not in
session, and apparently for the devil of it, pick up a rock, throw it,
and break out a window light. Of course every teacher who ever
taught there had to take the school water bucket home with her
every afternoon; otherwise somebody would be sure to steal it.)

Anyhow, the school board sent Miss Cora out to teach at that incorrigible school—with her one arm, dyed red hair, and all. When she hitched her horse and buggy out front, the students all began to giggle; it would not take them long to dispose of her they thought. They were wrong. She marched into the classroom with her buggy whip and a pistol, laid them on the desk, announced that she had come to teach, and that all who did not like it could leave right then. They all shaped up, and she stayed there until she decided to move on to other fields and pastures new and ended up at Maple Grove.

In those days teachers were paid little indeed: forty dollars a month was considered a good salary. But they usually got their "maintenance" as we would call it today by being boarded around at each of the families' homes in the community. I do not think Miss Cora ever lived with the Drakes, however. Why, I am not sure except that perhaps, with such a large family, there simply was no room for her. In fact, now that I look back on it, it seems to me that she never lived in the Maple Grove community at all but drove back and forth from Woodville, her home, every day. But they all got exposed to her at the school, and many were the tales they had to tell about her.

For one thing, though she believed in letting her students play and play hard outside the classroom, in there she meant strictly business and nobody had better have any other ideas. With strict justice she rewarded virtue (she gave Daddy a tie that she had knitted herself, though how she managed to do that with only one arm I do not know, when he memorized the multiplication table) and punished vice (the unruly got a thump on the head from the thimble she wore on her forefinger because she often did embroidery while they recited to her—and again how she managed that I do not know—or else they got a lick from her blackboard pointer across their backsides if they were really misbehaving). Absolutely no foolishness was allowed in her classroom; again as over in the next county, she had come to Maple Grove to teach school, and she intended to do it. Indeed, in later life, Miss Cora Jordan, in her unswerving devotion to the cause of education, became something of a symbol for me. In 1970, during the riots and disruptions on American university campuses, I happened to encounter, on a walk across the campus, one of the deans at the university where I was teaching. By way of cheering him up during those dark days and, incidentally, making known to him my own feelings—pretty strong ones—in the matter, I recounted to him the episode of Miss Cora and the buggy whip and pistol and ended with a sort of exhortation or battle cry: "Remember Miss Cora Jordan!" He got the point.

I do not know whether Miss Cora was more feared than admired by her students and their parents. In later years, they all conceded that she was a first-rate teacher who could almost teach students against their wills. (And indeed, how many of them ever really wanted to learn; how many in any class do?) She was not the sort of teacher—or the sort of woman—that one could ever get close to. She ran her school by what Jane Austen once called the strict rule of right, rewarding virtue and punishing vice with magisterial judgment; above all, she *taught* in that school. But was that enough for Maple Grove? Apparently it was not because somewhere along the line, after her first year there, a whispering campaign about her was initiated—nothing definite exactly except that, when all was said and done, she was something of a *high-stepper*. After all, she had dyed hair (who knew how old she might be?), and "nice" women did not dye their hair in those days. She always drove a first-rate horse, a *real* high-stepper, to her spanking fresh and clean buggy, and she lived in Woodville rather than boarding around in the Maple Grove community. She apparently did not have much to say about the everyday facts of Maple Grove life (did she consider herself superior to them?). She never really got "close" to anybody: she neither invited confidences nor gave them herself. She was there to teach and that was it.

Really, I do not know what the whispering campaign could actually say about her. Her private life was spotless as far as anybody knew. Occasionally, after school, Mr. Ben Edwards, an old bachelor who was supposed to be an atheist or at least an agnostic but owned a lot of land at Maple Grove, would ride up on his fine horse to call on her at the schoolhouse, and sometimes he would take her driving in his new buggy on the weekends. These actions could hardly be considered scandalous; after all, Miss Cora had survived thus far with only one arm and dyed red hair, so she could presumably take care of herself. Mr. Edwards of course never darkened the door of the Maple Grove Methodist Church, and that was a strike against him. Miss Cora, on the other hand, was supposed to be a Methodist, at least in Woodville, and it was said she always kept her pledge paid. One could not fault her on those grounds.

What, then, was the real trouble? Did her high-stepping mainly give offense, not because she flouted the proprieties or came into open conflict with Maple Grove, but simply because she did just that—stepped so high that she practically took no notice of Maple Grove at all? They could have warmed to her had she asked their advice, consulted them, humbled herself to them, even come to open war with them. That would at least have made her human; they could have understood and forgiven all that. Perhaps it never occurred to her to do so; she was there to teach school and nothing else. Her mental arithmetic drills and Friday afternoon spelling matches became, for Maple Grove, the terrors of the earth.

I do not think the Drakes as a family ever "took against" her. Pa was too easy-going and Grandma too charitable for that. But perhaps they did not spring all that readily to her defense either. I know that Pa did tell somebody that he respected anybody who believed in his job the way Miss Cora apparently believed in hers; she was really dedicated, he said. The thing was, she had nothing else to do with Maple Grove after that; she never called on her "patrons," as the parents of school children were then called, nor did she ever visit in their homes. She taught the children, sent messages to their parents when they needed new books or new clothes, told them by notes and letters when they needed to make their children work harder ("make them apply themselves," she said) or behave better in school ("teach them some manners," "make them show their raising," she called it). But she came no closer to them, or to Maple Grove, than that.

That was apparently what they could not forgive. The one arm, the dyed red hair, even the atheist or agnostic suitor (if such he was) they could have taken in their stride; but she *stepped too high* for them. Not that she ever implied, in her dealings with them, that she thought herself above them, either socially or in educational background, but her job there, to her way of thinking, seemed to be first and foremost and nothing whatsoever must be allowed to get in the way of that. She hated ignorance and often spoke of her work, with some irony, as healing the sick and raising the dead; but even more than that she hated laziness and lack of ambition (that was when she would speak of cleansing the lepers and casting out demons). She wanted her students to "amount to something,"—if it came to that, to get away from Maple Grove into the big wide world, she said, not that she necessarily looked down on Maple Grove, but mainly because she wanted all her students to "realize their lives," as she put it, to follow their individual stars, wherever they led. Most of her students never forgot her—stern mistress that she was—or her hopes for them, her ambitions. She once told Uncle Buford he would make a first-rate doctor because he was so sensitive to the feelings of others and hated suffering so much. As an old man, years later, I heard him tell somebody that he had always wanted to be a doctor, but, back in those days, where was the money for his education to come from?

What Maple Grove could not forgive in Miss Cora was the threat to the community they thought she posed. (And in some ways, of course, she did.) Thus began the whispering campaign: she was being courted (and perhaps more than courted) by an atheist; she was an atheist herself. Nothing definite was established, but vague, insubstantial rumors and idle talk circulated. Finally the county school board, who after all were elected to office, removed Miss Cora from her post at the end of her second year there.

Was she hurt, bewildered, perplexed? Nobody ever knew, certainly nobody out at Maple Grove. Again, that was perhaps part of her trouble and had been all along: she worked but she did not talk. In any case, she merely went back to teaching in the next county, where she had straightened out that disorderly school some years before. She did tell one of her friends in Woodville, though, that sometimes, in spite of all she had preached and practiced all her life, she thought it was almost a mistake to try to educate some people because, once that was done, they would look around them and see what a miserable condition their lives and their world were in and so perhaps the best thing to do in such cases was simply to leave them alone: ignorance was often bliss, she said. When people at Maple

Grove heard that, some of them did not know what to make of it but said, well, she was only a lonely, disappointed old maid and that explained everything about her. A few others, Pa and Grandma among them, said that there were some things in this world that were perfectly true and that anybody who was not a born fool knew them perfectly well but because they were so terrible to contemplate the less said about them, the better. Pa, in particular, said that when you came right down to it, there was nothing like *folks* anyhow.

❧ Grandma

My father and his brothers called their mother "Ma" and their father "Pa" which I used to think very tacky until I learned more about older life and ways in the South—mainly from reading *Gone With The Wind,* where the O'Hara girls, appropriately for the times, called their own parents by those names. In the back of my mind, I usually thought of her simply as "Grandma" because I never knew her and let it go at that. But always, for the Drake brothers themselves, she was "Ma." And they had all adored her.

Her name was Elizabeth Ann Burks, but I think Pa (I did actually call him that because I knew him: he lived until I was nearly eight) and everyone else in the community at Maple Grove called her Betty. I have been told that, if I had been a girl, I would have been named for her: Elizabeth Currie, with the latter name in remembrance of my maternal grandfather. Of course, I always thought of her as an old woman; Pa was ninety-two when he died, and I could not imagine her anything but old, too. Actually she was sixty-two at the time of her death, in those days considered the age of an old woman, I believe. They all said she had literally worked herself to death for her husband and five sons. Her two daughters had died and she had grieved inordinately over the untimely death of Eashel, the younger one, who was her pride and joy.

I suspect, of course, that both accounts of her death were correct. Her love made her spend herself utterly for her family, but, by the same token, her love made her more susceptible to any loss from that quarter. Grandma had worked and had indeed loved her life away, to hear them tell it. She must have been a wonderful woman, but somehow I never resented her wonderfulness as I did Eashel's. I used to hear so much about Eashel's perfections that I became weary of the whole idea: surely no one could ever have been that beautiful, that talented, and that good. Grandma was not similarly held as a paragon of all virtues. Why? For one thing, she lived long enough to more or less realize her life: one could never sit around and ponder on what she might have done if only she had lived. She had raised a fine family, and she had served her husband devotedly.

Still I felt deprived for not having known her. Pa was the only one of my grandparents I actually ever knew, and I was envious of my friends and playmates who had four living grandparents to love and be spoiled by. I felt cheated: I ought to have had a grandmother in my life, I knew. Surely, her existence would have opened new horizons for me, given me a new perspective on the whole family and my place in it, to say nothing of giving me a firmer grasp on understanding the generations of men—how my parents had themselves been children and thus had no absolute stranglehold on authority and power. It always made me come up with a start to think that my parents were themselves someone else's children and had to conduct themselves accordingly. Perhaps that is difficult enough for anyone to imagine, but I felt deprived, as I said, and wished very much that I could have known Grandma.

I have often wondered what her own family was like. I used to wonder privately whether Pa had considered his marriage to her beneath him. Of course I have no overt evidence for such a specula-tion at all, but he had come to Tennessee from his home in Virginia and his family had been well-to-do landholders who had owned slaves. He had been sent off to school to an "academy," from which he ran away to join the Confederate Army, and I gather that he had come from good folks. He was an aristocrat in his looks and in his demeanor. I remember his looks—the aquiline profile and the tall slim figure erect and proud (until he broke his hip). I have heard about his demeanor—imperious and peremptory on occasion—and often he was not terribly easy to get along with, especially as he grew older.

Grandma was apparently the wheel behind the wheel there. She was a worker in her house and garden and all that concerned her family; certainly she never took a seat to talk over old times and old ways, as Pa was reputed to have done. In fact, I have often wondered whether, with all due respects to everybody concerned, Pa was not naturally lazy. Yes, I know he must have had to come down from the slave-holding days, to make all the adjustments everybody had to in those days but I suspect there was something of a constitutional weakness there, too. About Grandma's reminiscences, however, I never heard a word: she apparently was not much of a talker or else did not have much time to be. Perhaps it all comes down to the same thing.

Anyhow, I cannot be sure that Grandma was "beneath" Pa. They lived on her little farm, the home place, and it was she who kept things going. If some of her own kinfolks—the ones I knew later on—seemed a little on the tacky side, perhaps that was a result of my own lack of understanding. They apparently had been landholders all along, though I suspect they never owned many slaves. I imagine now that they were part of the large body of yeoman farmers who populated the South both before and after the war, living on their own small farms but with no high flying, beholden to nobody in this world, and fiercely independent. Again, this is mostly surmise on my part. But the other members of her family I came to know later on, mostly cousins, were not people of any worldly ambition. They were well content to occupy whatever niche Providence had placed them in and seemingly had no higher aspirations. A number of them even intermarried with the Woods, my mother's family, though she and my father were not actually kin to each other. The Woods were not long on the things I had come to value like eduation and self-improvement though, like my father's family, they were people capable of great affection and feeling. However, as someone has remarked of such folk, they did not *talk* about the good life; they simply *lived* it. That construction is certainly possible, as I look back on all of them now, and there is a lot to be said for it, too, certainly in the light of our characteristic American middle-class itch to let us then be up and doing. (Of course, as some wise soul has long since pointed out, Longfellow never did prescribe *what* it was we were to do; and there lies the rub.)

Was that one reason why I always felt uneasy in the presence of talk about Grandma? That it somehow was she, the more humbly born of the two, who kept things going, who really raised the family, who made possible the life they led, the affections they shared—she who had not the background and the manner that Pa certainly had. Did I somehow resent her living the good life rather than talking about it? Did I feel this was a reflection on Pa and his background in the Old Dominion? Was her life too narrow, too confined for anything like wider knowledge, much less sophistication? Was I even perhaps a little ashamed of her?

I have often wondered about these things. She was apparently literate, but I never heard of her indulging any particular taste for literature, and it is possible that her reading was confined to the Bible and the Sunday school quarterly. Think of this: she was never on a train in her life! We can hardly imagine such a thing, and certainly the Drakes were something of a traveling group, for those days. Pa went back to Virginia several times for Confederate reunions and to see his family there, and Eashel went with him. Uncle John had even gone to school for a brief time in Texas and later to the Vanderbilt Divinity School. Daddy went to New York to market and to New Haven, Connecticut, to attend a Winchester Repeating Arms convention, after of course he was out in the world and established in the hardware business. By the time I came along, however, neither he nor my mother ever expressed much interest in travel (it would not have bothered either one of them to be told they could never leave the county again), whereas, as long as I can remember, I very much wanted to go places and see the sights. Grandma's never riding on a train is incredible to me. Surely, one might argue, she must have gone to Memphis to shop; surely there were people there she wanted to see. But it was not so. She could do all the shopping her time and her means allowed in Woodville, and whom did she have to visit away from home? All her family lived right there in that one county. Where was there, really, for her to go? Today it is difficult for us to imagine such a life, but I never heard that she was dissatisfied in any way with hers.

But again, what passions, what desires might have been hers, if her circumstances had been different? For all I know, she might have longed desperately to get away, to try herself in the wider world; but the conventions of the day, the exigencies of her home and family life must have made any such thoughts seem not only out of the question but downright treasonable as well. I cannot be certain, for no evidence exists in support of these conjectures. In some ways, she seems colorless; few anecdotes were told about her (not nearly so many as about Pa), and I never heard much about what she said in casual conversation as they sat on the front porch or around the dinner table. Perhaps these voids are indicative too of her having no time for such matters; her work was too pressing. (Aunt Estelle said Grandma never kept a servant because nobody could please her as far as housekeeping went—not even Eashel, whom she would not trust to churn when she was away from home once on a brief visit to Uncle John and Aunt Estelle. She told Eashel to see that the cow was milked but to throw the milk away!) Yet she must have given all her family a great love: they all adored her, as I have said. Later, when they were all old men, they could scarcely talk about her without tears. They could not have been so moved had she not given them a great deal. That is the enigma of Grandma. On the one hand, I used to feel that I had heard entirely too much about Eashel—that all the family were, knowingly or not, trying to turn her into a legend—but I never felt that I knew enough about Grandma, except of course how much they all loved her. Was that her reward, and was it enough to be carried so long afterwards in memory and in love?

Pa, on the other hand, was very different indeed, and the tales about him were legion, especially as he got older. But then he had the time, rather he took the time, to be remembered. He was very colorful too, with a mind and a will that could not have been changed with a sledgehammer. Grandma, I gather, was, especially with outsiders, shy and diffident. Did she feel that a woman's place was merely that of the center of the family and was she content with that? Many people today might find such a status not to their taste, but I never heard anything to indicate that she found it offensive. In the family photographs, of which a good many survive, Grandma is always half-hidden behind somebody (they said she always hated having her picture taken) as if reluctant to put herself forward. She looks not meek but perhaps serene there. Surely, though, she must have known who she was and where she was and, even more important, where she was going. Her eyes and the thrust of her chin indicate as much there. Quiet and retiring she may well have been when confronted with the wide world, but, as someone else has said, it was enough for her, like many women of that time, to *be* rather than to *do*.

Thus the color surrounding Grandma was mostly provided by Pa and a few members of her own family—"Aunt," for instance. Aunt, who was Grandma's aunt, later became the second wife of my mother's grandfather and thus further complicated relationships between the two families. Theirs was "one of those Wood–Burks arrangements," as one of the cousins somewhat peremptorily dismissed it. Grandma always taught all her family that Aunt was the finest cook in the world and the best housekeeper. There were many tales about her and my Great-grandfather Wood. Once when asked who had ironed the clothes, which apparently were not so crisply done as they should have been, she observed drily that "Susan"—a colored servant?—"had *folded* the clothes." Another time, when my great-grandfather had come into town to buy a new suit of clothes, he took one look at himself in the new three-way mirror and somewhat querulously asked, "Adeline, why didn't you tell me I was bow-legged?" She replied, "I've been knowing it for twenty years but never thought it worth saying anything about."

I do not feel that I have come to terms with Grandma very well here, for there seems so little to tell. Yet perhaps the key to her whole character is that nothing happened to her. Her life was thoroughly quiet and domestic, and she stayed at home and looked after her family. She never went anywhere; she never did anything; yet she was apparently loving and much beloved. My father told me that when he went home for the last time to see her before her death he sat for a long time before the fire, with his head in her lap, neither of them saying a word to each other, perhaps sensing that words would be useless on what might be their last time together. In fact, I gather that with Grandma words were always somehow superfluous. I have heard few things she ever said, and even fewer anecdotes told about what she did. Again, she simply *was*, and who among us now can say that she did not thereby realize her life?

When I was home for Christmas some years ago—a dozen, I guess it was—Uncle Buford, with whom I always stayed after my parents had died, remarked, seemingly apropos of nothing, that the following morning would mark the fiftieth anniversary of Grandma's death (he even gave me the exact time but I have forgotten it). I marveled then that, after all those years, her death—and her life—could still mean so much to him. But now that I am nearly twelve years older, I do not wonder at it at all any more.

❧ *The Picture Frame*

MY FATHER'S OLDEST BROTHER, Uncle John, was a Methodist preacher and an avid photographer. In fact, my mother said he had been taking pictures so long that he must have had a camera since the year one. I believe she looked askance at his picture-taking. I am not altogether sure why except perhaps she thought it too expensive and time-consuming a sideline for a dedicated minister of the Gospel. I suppose my father had reservations about it, too, though he never made himself known directly in the matter. I do know, however, that he steadfastly refused all my entreaties to be given a camera for Christmas when I was growing up, and I could not understand why. Surely, it was a harmless enough diversion. And it was fun to see how the photographs all turned out after they had been made.

I never had a camera until I was grown, and all the technical jargon made me think it might be too difficult for me to master, even after I was making my own money. Also, I made fun of the tourists who never saw anything of Europe or the Grand Canyon except what they were able to get inside the camera lens. I thought that was no way to travel. A camera might be fun, but it should be kept in its place.

My father and the other Drakes indulged Uncle John in his one real folly by buying the prints he made (he did his own developing) of family gatherings and so on, the scenes he took of the church, the graveyard, the old home place at Maple Grove, now idle and empty, or anything else old, dead, and buried. His photography was a financial drain, I imagine now, that Uncle John on his preacher's salary could ill afford. One such indulgence, however, was enough.

51

For me to take up photography must have been more than my father could bear to contemplate, and for that reason I went without a camera until I was well into adulthood. Then I settled for the "instamatic" kind that either worked or did not. I still do not want to photograph scenery, which you can always buy on picture post cards better than you can take. Instead, I want to make pictures of my friends and their houses, the people and places that have happened to me, the personal and the immediate. I think, in that way, I am like Uncle John, who always wanted to set things down, either in writing (he kept a diary for forty years) or on film, "for the record," as he said. Whenever there was an argument or some dispute about a fact, a place, or a person amongst the brothers, who all lived in that one county and saw each other frequently, Uncle John could settle it by appealing to the record. What would he think now, when most people I know proclaim, "I never write letters," with the same smugness that they would say, "I don't rob banks" or "I don't forge checks"? One apparently is supposed to be dumbfounded and not a little awed by such a categorical assertion. How busy they must be, how many affairs they must have on hand, how pressed for time they sound, never to be able to indulge in putting pen to epistolary paper!

Perhaps, though, they are not as busy as they would have one think; they may all be like Chaucer's Man of Law, who "ever seemed busier than he was." Always part of an act or a facade, such a statement makes me angry. It suggests the speaker simply is not willing to take the time that letter-writing requires and further implies that he does not think the would-be recipient of the letter is worth the effort. What will the historian of the future have for his primary sources now that letter-writing has pretty much gone by the board? Will he have to rely on that murky phenomenon known as "oral history," which can be extremely unreliable, filtered as it is through other times, other memories, and perhaps rearranged years after the fact to suit the informant's particular whim or predilections? How valid will their records be then? Will they really be records at all?

I know what Uncle John and the other Drakes would probably say: they would not give any of it the time of day as far as being an authoritative record was concerned. Records, as contrasted with

*The author's father is flanked in this photograph, taken
around the close of the nineteenth century, by two of his
brothers: Buford (left) and Jim (right).*

memories, were what one put down at the time, the way things
actually happened, the way things really were—at least to him.
They might be thin or inadequate, but at least they were his own,
and they told the truth as far as he could tell it. Thus they had a
measure of authority which would be denied memories recollected
long after the fact.

This is not to say the Drakes did not cherish—and relish—the
spoken word, the living memory. They did very much. I realize now
that this was one of their greatest treasures—and one of my greatest
resources—both as a tale-teller and as a man. But the spoken
memories were subject to change, subject to being formed and
shaped and therefore, to some extent, suspect as history pure and
simple, if there ever is any such animal. The spoken word was, for
them, the world where their affections lived—their hopes, their
fears, their sorrows, their joys—the world where they reentered the
past, re-created it on the spot, and summoned it up, like Lazarus
from the dead. There it came to them on their own terms, and there
they were safe with it.

But with pictures, diaries, and records it was otherwise. They
were sometimes prosy, even dull. In photographs all was revealed in

the light of common day, as it were. The sister who had died young looks sweet but is no great beauty in the photographs. Of course her character cannot be discerned there. My father, I know, adored her—her and his mother, in particular—and in later years could hardly ever speak of either of them without tears: the sister, who had died so out of time, and the mother, who, to his way of thinking, had worked and grieved herself to death. In the photographs, again, my grandmother looks tiny, shy, defenseless perhaps; but something of the granite is also discernible. Her spirit seems to shine through— a "stayer"—if only her body would acquiesce, but she died at sixty-two.

Did the camera lie about either of them? Perhaps not. It simply did all any camera could do by recording what it saw. The rest would have to lie in memory, in the spoken word, where they were all conjured up from the blessed dead, the terrible past. Could such memories, so personal, so partial, be trusted? On the other hand, was not something of a blessing present in them even when they might have been refined through several layers of gauze, seen through spectacles more than rose-colored? Was this not a grace which the remembered past bestowed, and was it not indeed a saving grace, to some extent? Do we, after all, really want "the record," as Uncle John called it, kept straight? Sometimes, historians tell us, what actually happened is not so important as what people think happened. Perhaps this is what the Drakes kept safe in their innumerable tales and recollections about the family, for in them they were safe; the record, on the other hand—the pictures, the diaries—might pull them back, set the record straight. From it there was no appeal, but in some measure the same was true of their tales also: who could say them nay when they were thus summoning up those old people, those old times? Perhaps, to some extent, both the record and the memory were true—the difference between fact and fiction—both equally true but true in a different way, perhaps with equal authority, both equally necessary in the world of the Drakes.

One thing you notice again and again, though, in the old family photographs is how many people are crowded into them. To be sure, Uncle John liked to photograph individuals (he was even called in on

*Pa Drake, who died in 1938, in one of the
last of Uncle John's photographs of him.*

occasion to photograph dead people in their coffins so their families
could remember how they looked when they were laid away), but he
liked nothing as much as a group picture, especially a family group,
and no family more than the Drakes. It was as though there he could
squeeze them all together into one picture frame, into some sort of
little world, could put them all together so they would never, for the
moment, be parted, never know the pangs of separation which must
and would come in time—as though he were striking some sort of
private bargain with God. ("Just let me get them all together one
more time, all under one roof, for the record, and then You may do
as You please.") And there they would be, teeming with life and
vitality and about to explode from the picture frame.

When I used to have to pose for the group pictures at Christmas
dinners and so on I thought it all a big bore. For one thing, Uncle
John would keep us waiting outside in the freezing cold for what
seemed like hours while he disappeared under the black cloth to see
whether everybody was in focus. When I was young, it always
scared me a little to see Uncle John, whom I knew and loved as well
as anybody, be half-transmuted into a figure of terror by going under

Top: *The author is pictured standing, third from the left, at a Drake Christmas dinner held in the late 1940s.*

Bottom: *The Drakes, preserved for "the record" in this 1950 photograph, at a family gathering held at Uncle Wesley's.*

the black cloth. O, yes, I knew it was he all the time, but still. . . . What did he become when he laid aside his avuncular, to say nothing of his ministerial, role for that of the dispassionate recorder and photographer? Was there not something of the bloodless, even

"In the group pictures, we are all there as though Uncle John had literally gone out into the highways and byways and compelled us to come in for 'the record.'"

the sinister about it? Now, of course, nothing so dramatic happens. One just smiles hard, perhaps even says "cheese," and the instamatic clicks; then, as I said, it either works or does not. Worst of all used to be the indoor photographs, complete with exploding powder to provide the light—a terrible thrill at birthday parties when I was growing up. Now of course it is only a brief flash from a "cube," and that is that.

In the group pictures, we are all there as though Uncle John had literally gone out into the highways and byways and compelled us to come in for "the record." Sometimes, there would even be a stray neighbor or two: Uncle John—and all the Drakes, for that matter—were great includers rather than excluders. They wanted as many folks in the group as possible, family or not. It was like a great free Communion of the Saints and open to all. In that time and place, families were, I believe, one or the other, and many of the ones I knew were excluders: clannish, "me and mine," and the rest of the world could go and be damned. But not so with the Drakes. Loving one another so deeply, secure in the affection so freely bestowed, never feeling that the well might or could run dry, they wanted to bring the whole wide world into their circle and into the photographs if it could be done. Really, I think, they almost did, but not of course in any tangible way; they never left much mark on the surface of their world. They left no sizeable "estates"; they accumulated little worldly goods. But what memories, what love they left behind! They could love one another, whether living or dead, without reservation; but they seemed to be capable of loving beyond the family too.

I often hear when I go home, "Your Daddy and your Uncle Buford—the ones in business together so long,—why, they were just like fathers to me. They helped me get my start. What this world needs is more men like them. What this world needs is more Drakes!" The first time I heard it, I almost wept, for joy, for gratitude, to think that my father and all of them should be so kindly remembered. ("O, how we all loved Brother Drake when he was our pastor!" They often spoke of Uncle John and the others, too.) But I had grown older, had grown up, since I used to hate to freeze to death on the front steps while Uncle John disappeared under the black hood to make those group pictures. I was beginning to understand what a priceless legacy the Drakes had left me, though not in anything tangible. Yes, the records were there: the diaries, the letters, the pictures most of all. More important, though, were the memories, the myths even, that they had spawned and fostered, the closeness of family, the fidelity of friends, the oneness of the whole wide world—so capable they seemed of taking it all in within the vast splendor of their love. It was the whole world, finally, that was their picture frame. But it was not until you had stepped outside it in some way, gone away to foreign places, alien lands near or far, that you could know that, realize what you had been given and were still being given in their memories, their legacy, their love.

2

MY FATHER AND MY MOTHER

MY MOTHER, who was Lillian Wood, was born in 1890 at Maple Grove, where my father grew up. I think their families had always known each other, but were never close friends, and my parents did not really meet, you might say, until they were grown. However, they remembered things about each other's families all their lives. My father recalled that it was my maternal grandmother who had taught him his first memory verse to recite at the Children's Day exercises at the Maple Grove Methodist Church. He also remembered a flustered preacher, during the rehearsals, who was uncertain about the choreography of his movements on the platform and turned to my Grandmother Wood and asked, rather plaintively, "Miss Ella, where shall I appear from?" My mother also recollected that she had seen "Betty" Drake, my other grandmother, driving a buggy down the road, had asked who she was, and had been told. There was no other direct intercourse between the families as far as I know.

My mother's family moved to town, out to Woodville, around 1894, and for a time they lived at the county jail because my grandfather, Currie Wood, was serving as jailer for his cousin who was sheriff then, "Uncle Bob" Wood, as my mother always called him. Daddy used to tease Mamma about having lived in the jail when she first came to town, but she would reply that, at any rate, she had gotten out of the country before he did and had been exposed to a modicum of civilization while she was still young enough for it to take. He would never make any reply to this except to smile, shake his head, and observe that you could not get ahead of Mamma.

After a couple of years there, the Woods moved from the jail to a house my grandfather bought on what would later be called Jefferson Street; it was the house where I later was born and lived all my life until I went away to school. There were four in my mother's family: my mother, her brother, and her parents. Another brother had died as a little boy, and all I ever saw of him was a fading old photograph that Mamma had put into a handsome old walnut frame; the frame was really more impressive than he was, I always thought. He may have been fortunate in the time of his death, for it occurred at an early age, before life really got hold of him.

The Woods and the Drakes—or rather the Burkses, Grandma Drake's family—had intermarried a great deal; but strangely enough, although my parents were often kin to the same people, but on different sides of the house, as we say, they were not kin to each other. Daddy said he always remembered Mamma as the pretty little girl with blue eyes who was full of mischief and so sweet and pretty you wanted to hug and kiss her right away. Such flattery, however, went only so far with Mamma who said, whenever Daddy talked that way, he was only trying to pull the wool over her eyes about something he did not want her to know. Still, she liked it for what it was but did not hesitate to take Daddy down a peg or two when he got too big for his breeches, especially when he teased her about getting old; she reminded him that no matter how old she was, he was always five years older. Then later she would observe that her father had been younger than Daddy was right then when he died and that he had been considered an old man. That was supposed to take care of Daddy, but of course it never did.

My mother had had sorrow in her life while she was still fairly young. For one thing, she lost both her parents within six weeks of each other: her mother had had gall bladder surgery in Memphis and had died of complications, and her father had died a few weeks later of a stroke. I naturally wondered what they were like: they, along with Grandma Drake, had all died in 1917, many years before I was born. All I could get out of most of the family—the Woods, at any rate—was that they had been fine, upstanding people, beloved members of the community. That did not tell me very much. I did hear that my Grandmother Wood, who had been born Ella Cobb, was considered by many to be "peculiar" and not very outgoing: she mostly stayed at home, found there her center of life and work apparently and, indeed, hardly ever went to church. On the other hand, my grandfather, Currie Wood, was very much the hail-fellow-well-met: for years until his death, almost without interruption, he served as town marshal. He was much beloved by old and young alike, white and black, nearly all of whom called him by his first name. My mother of course had adored him and liked to fancy that she was very much like him, especially in the sunny disposition for which he had been famous. Some of her cousins later told me that this was not so; she grew more like her mother every day, they said.

Therefore, although my mother and father were aware of each other, they had never been really thrown together until after her home was broken up by the death of her parents and she went to live up at her Aunt Hattie's. Aunt Hattie was married to Grandma Wood's brother, Uncle Ben, and she had kept a boarding house for some years. Sooner or later, it seemed that every single, unattached person, male or female, who ever passed through Woodville went to live up there. Aunt Hattie received Mamma with open arms, and Mamma liked it well enough. She said the one thing she could not stand was that Aunt Hattie always had canned vegetables on the table even in the summertime when they were growing practically right outside the door. Of course a full complement of old-maid school teachers was always on hand, as well as sales clerks in the downtown stores, with occasionally an itinerant milliner passing through to liven things up. Life up at Aunt Hattie's could not have been very exciting, though I think from the tales Mamma and Daddy used to tell about the days "when we were living together before we were married!" it must have been fun.

Daddy had come into town about 1908, I believe, the year that Mamma graduated from high school, to work in Mr. Randolph's hardware store, and he lived up at Aunt Hattie's; that was where they began their courtship, after Mamma moved up there in 1917. Daddy had courted other ladies, to be sure, and I once heard that he had given one of them a diamond engagement ring. I know that my mother had had at least one other serious suiter—a Mr. Jamieson, who was a Methodist preacher and a graduate of the University of North Carolina. (He used to send her crates of blueberries on occasion.) Somehow my parents felt that there was no one else for them but each other, and they were married in 1922, when my mother was thirty-two and my father thirty-seven.

They first had rooms at another boarding house in Woodville, while Mamma's house on Jefferson Street was being remodeled for them, but they soon were able to move in there, and there they remained for all their married life; it lasted until my father died in 1957. A few years after his death my mother went into a decline from which she never really recovered and ultimately had to be confined to a state psychiatric hospital, dying, finally, after a long illness of both mind and body in 1968. She had had other sieges of mental illness, the first of them when I was in my early teens and she was going through menopause. Her story does not seem like a very happy one here; certainly, it is at some variance with that of the Drakes, who I think knew sorrow very well but not real agony.

And yet no one could be more charming than my mother when she was well and happy, which she often was in my childhood, and no one could be more fun. She loved being teased, and my father loved to tease her. One of his favorite jests had to do with her diamond ring, which was the only really good piece of jewelry she ever owned. It was a beautiful solitaire in a Tiffany mounting, and interestingly enough he had not given it to her on their engagement. She had, rather, bought it with her own money, as an investment, some time before they were married. One of my mother's pet peeves, for many years, was someone's—a widow or widower usually—having his name put on a tombstone beside his spouse or other close relative before his death, just to have all in readiness presumably. My mother said she could not abide such beforehand zeal; death would come soon enough without rushing things, she said. My father would tease her about her beautiful diamond and end up always by saying that he knew when I got married she would want to give her ring to my wife. My mother would swell up and announce as

something final and settled, without hope of amendment or appeal, that there were two things she never expected to see during her lifetime: her name on a tombstone and her diamond ring on another woman's hand. And that was that. My father would be highly amused of course, and she would be, too. But she meant every word of it.

They seemed a fairly well-matched pair to me, and certainly as raconteurs they were a superb team. My father was blustery and bold, my mother more delicate and sly. Their life together must always remain something of a puzzle to me, their only child. Why did they marry? Why do anyone's parents ever marry? In some ways, they seemed ill suited to each other; in other ways, they were very compatible indeed. My mother remained always, for my father, the little girl with the blue eyes he had seen at the Children's Day service so long ago, I think, and for her, he was husband and lover but, more importantly, I believe, the father she had lost so early. (She often called him "Daddy," though that was only after I was born, I believe.) My father delighted in spoiling her, and she very much enjoyed being spoiled.

She fitted into the world of the Drakes very well, though later on I think they found it difficult to be entirely sympathetic with her "nervousness" (they were not "nervous" people themselves). They loved her gaiety and her wit; they loved her stories and her fun.

Above all, they loved her cooking. (She was the best cook in a family that really relished its food.) And it was she who began the institution of the famous Drake dinners at Christmastime, when we would have not one but five such dinners (one at each brother's house) over a period of two weeks' time. (Mamma always led off with her dinner on the Sunday before Christmas.) O, what food there was on the table then, with each of the wives vying in the friendliest possible way to see who could put the finest spread before us! How outsiders used to tease us about the "Drake Christmas dinners," as they were called when they were written up in the society column of the local newspaper! We knew they were all halfway envious too—envious of our good tables but perhaps as much envious of what our family really cherished about those times, the warmth and the intimacy they all held.

Of course I looked forward to the dinners almost as much as to Santa Claus: the excitement, the smells, the tastes, even, as I grew older, the Drake tales, which were never told with more relish or more gusto than at the dinners. As a little boy, too, I loved the excitement of seeing my Grandmother Wood's big banquet cloth laid out on the old oak dinner table that Daddy said all the Drakes had fought around when they were growing up; and then her hand-embroidered napkins would be placed there, twelve of them, complete with the big Old English "W" she had worked on each one. And there would be Mamma's French Haviland china with the scalloped gold band, too, but I never got to eat off it; there were settings for only twelve, and all the grown folks took up the room there. We cousins all had to eat at card tables in Mamma and Daddy's bedroom, and I thus felt always somewhat left out. (One time I was so dispirited that Daddy brought me his Haviland plate and took my own "everyday" plate back to the big table himself.) I reveled in this great annual flowering of the Drakes, and one of the Drake aunts has told me that she remembers my standing at the entrance to the dining room to exclude all the Woods (the few members of Mamma's family that she always invited) until all the Drakes were seated!

The dinners came to an end shortly before the death of my father, as the brothers began to die off and the survivors began to succumb to the infirmities of age. By this time my mother was unwell, too;

The Drake brothers, seated chronologically from left to right, at a family dinner in December of 1950.

indeed she would never be really sound in mind and body again. That was part of her tragedy; whereas my father had literally dropped dead (one morning at the breakfast table), it seemed as though she could not die. I had to watch her withdraw more and more into a private, institutional world of her own, and few things can be sadder than that, I believe. When she was in her prime, she had very much entered into the Drake world, though she was never entirely of it. The surviving Drakes missed her I think. She would always refer to things that had happened before or after the time when she "came into the family," and I felt that being a Drake was very important to her, too, even if only by marriage. There were differences between them; there is no doubt about that. Did some of the Drakes feel that she constituted some sort of threat to their kind of family life, she who had never known and never found in the family what they had always cherished there? After all, her own family had been broken up early. Did they feel that, in some ways, she and my father were ill suited for each other? These are old, tired questions, the answers to which are impossible now and perhaps would be of no avail if they were known. But I have tried to come to terms with these and some other considerations in the selections which follow.

❧ Currie

"TRUE-HEARTED, WHOLE-HEARTED, NOBLE-HEARTED Currie Wood is dead," began his obituary in the Woodville paper. Then the article went on at some length to describe the sterling qualities of this man who, dead at only fifty-eight, for so many years had served as the town marshal. The burden of the account was how popular he had been with his fellow townspeople and how much beloved. That is what I think mainly catches and holds my interest about this man who was my maternal grandfather and whom I never knew. I read obituaries still today, and I often see that someone has been prominent in the community and active in any number of good works therein, but I never see that he has been *beloved*. I wonder whether that tells us something about our times or about ourselves.

I have heard all my life about how popular Currie Wood was with his fellow citizens—so popular that most of them, including the children of the community, merely called him "Currie," with no "Mr." or other title preceding. I gather this was in no way intended to show disrespect: there was simply no one else there like him, and therefore "Currie" was all that was needed. He was *sui generis*.

My mother, his only daughter, had loved him very much indeed, and after she was grown she took "Currie" as her middle name. She fancied, so I have been told, that she was like him, though I have heard that contradicted. (And thereby hangs another tale.) I understand, though not from her, that he sometimes called my mother "Coon"—a nickname I do not know the significance of though perhaps it might have something to do with my mother's dramatic and striking blue eyes. They were so blue they seemed almost to

66

Currie Wood.

smolder, like a raccoon's, with the color. Around me she always spoke of her father, with the greatest deference, as "Papa."

Occasionally, when she was feeling her oats a bit—perhaps even a bit feisty, you might say—she would sound as though she might have had too much of such an idol as he was, certainly too much of her son, whom she did indeed love very much too. She would suddenly exclaim, "I never have had any individuality of my own! When I was a little girl, I was always known as Currie Wood's daughter, and now I'm nothing but Robert Drake's mother!" Then she would draw herself up and look around the room to see whether anybody had noticed what she had said, draw in her lips, and look extremely satisfied with herself at having gotten that out of her system. At other times, she would hold her father over my father's head, to put the quietus on him when she thought he was getting too big for his breeches. She would get on a high horse and threaten to change my name to Currie Wood, to which my father's reply was always the same: "Well, he's got my hair and eyes and my name, and you can have the rest of him."

Everybody apparently loved Currie Wood and not just because of his job either, which he more than adequately performed. For one thing, he was always highly visible. Everybody in town recognized my grandfather's handsome gray stallion coming down the road; and, of course, grandly mounted thereon, he led every parade ever held in those parts. In more than one way, he literally lived up to his title of marshal because he was a born presider and manager. If someone had a daughter coming in on the late train from Memphis, he would ask my grandfather to be at the station to see that she got home all right, mainly to keep an eye on her until she was borne away by the station bus to her destination. Another time, he was down there when they brought Miss Anne Wilson, Mr. Andrew Wilson's wife, home from the sanitarium where nothing could be done for her consumption. My grandfather was there to meet the train and help to lift her on her stretcher out of the baggage car, where they carried invalids in those days; she looked up at him, to thank him for his kindness, and said, "Mr. Wood, I've come home to die." My grandfather thought that very sad indeed. He had the kindest heart in the world, everybody said. Even the Negroes had to admit that. When he caught them shooting craps or broke up a razor fight, he carried them off to jail, laughing at them all the while but firm nevertheless. In fact, they were about the only beings in town who did not call him "Currie" as a matter of course.

He was a great funeral-goer, too, which I have often noticed is characteristic of outgoing and public people and does not necessarily reflect any morbidity of mind. Indeed, my mother even said that that was how she got to know all her kinfolks: my grandfather would take her to all the funerals around in the county and introduce her to various cousins and in-laws or whatever, but then she never would see them again until the next funeral, the roads and the means of transportation being what they were in those days. He was often called on to be a pallbearer, too, and back then pallbearers wore white gloves as a customary thing. For years after his death, my mother said she used his old left-over pallbearer's gloves to do her housework in.

All this adds up to a portrait of a man who was apparently very loving and, in turn, very much beloved, but nothing in either literature or life is ever quite so simple as that. From all I gather, Currie (that is what I always called him in my private mind, as though trying to make up for not having been a child during his lifetime) had a difficult time at home with my grandmother. I do not mean to imply that they quarreled or had marital difficulties; indeed, all I know about their marital life is based on a handful of statements and inferences made by people outside the family—certainly never on anything from my mother. I gather that my grandmother was considered "peculiar" by many people in town: she hardly left home, she hardly ever went downtown, she hardly ever went to church. Did she find her whole life simply fulfilled at home, with no need to move in the world outside? Was she merely one of those domestic women who find the family their be-all and end-all, or was there something constitutionally amiss?

I know that she had had some dark moments in the past: she had been married before, and her husband had been killed in an accident and their little children had died. She was supposed to have had a nervous breakdown or something then. My mother never spoke of these things to me: I learned them from one of the old-maid cousins, who are often keepers of the holy mysteries in such a world. Somehow, there was always something to make me feel that everybody watched himself around my grandmother; no one wanted to upset her, I suppose. She had other peculiarities as well: she would tell my mother to go on and cook dinner while she finished making a dress for her, resulting in my mother's becoming a superb cook but never really learning to sew. Another time she refused to let one of the cousins, who was then a little girl, take home the funny paper because she had not finished reading all that issue yet—nothing really bizarre here, only curious, I suppose. And so I wondered whether or not my grandfather was trying to make up for some of her eccentricities in his own extrovert and gregarious behavior. Again, I have nothing to go on here. But again and again I meet people who tell me how fine my grandfather was and how much everyone loved him, and they invariably end by telling me, "I didn't know your grandmother very well, though."

Currie could be stern in his own way and in his own time. Once when one of his cousins from the next county wanted him to go "stand up" with him at his wedding, Currie refused because he did not approve of the character of the bride's father, who had once been married to one of his sisters but had not been kind to her and their children, all of whom later died. I gather that Currie never said much about it; he merely acted, and people could take it as they liked. They always said that his word was his bond too—about the highest compliment one could pay a man in those days, and in these, too, for that matter. (Does anyone ever hear it now?) O, there was backbone in him all right. He was not just a sweet old pet; that is for certain. Law and order were literally his business; and he had been elected to keep the peace, which he did, with no favors to anybody. Of course, there were inevitably detractors. I once heard it said that one of the queen dowagers of the town observed that Currie had such a red face (he did, which made him look like Santa Claus except that he had a mustache but no beard, my mother said) and was always so jolly, he must be drinking. But everybody knew how to take such comments: my mother remained furious about it, though, for the rest of her life, but nobody for a minute ever believed it. They considered the source too (a dessicated old hag) and took it all merely at face value.

I suspect now that Currie did have a red face for a very good reason; he must have had high blood pressure and heart trouble since he died of a stroke. He had the same service read by the same Methodist pastor, the same kind of white coffin, the same hymns—everything—at his funeral which my grandmother had had at hers six weeks earlier. I have often wondered about my mother in all this: she loved him so much, and he died when she was a young unmarried woman in her twenties. How alone she must have felt, with her only brother already married and with a home of his own. Was that why she seemed to want to hold onto Currie even from beyond the grave, with her insistence on how close she and "Papa" were, how much she loved him, how much she loved being his "Coon" (though never this last to me—did she consider the usage too intimate?)? She had had to be absent from him too during the last weeks of his life, nursing her mother in the hospital in Memphis. And did she somehow feel guilty about this? Never did she say how much she had loved her mother, though "Mamma" always figured very much in her conversation. It was always "Papa" that she *loved,* that she used that word about. Even then did she feel her mother's history of "peculiarity" and "nervousness" hanging over her? Was she trying to lay that specter by concentrating on Currie, who was apparently so joyfully alive and life-giving?

These are questions I have pondered for years, with no satisfactory answer—as there never is when we try to unlock the mysteries of the past. But I do know that I like to look back on Currie as my grandfather and think that, when I am being joyful and giving pleasure, whether in my work or in my private life, I must be showing signs of being his only grandson. He was a life-giver; that seems evident to me now. I have lived long enough to know that basically the world is divided into two classes of people: those who stand for life and those who stand for death. And there has never been any question in my mind where Currie stood. My mother used to say, "If only Papa had been alive, how much he would have loved you! He would have spoiled you rotten!" Strangely enough— perhaps blessedly enough—I have somehow felt something of him working in me nearly all my life: the gusto, the joy, the celebration for which he must have stood. And though I never knew him, I think I have loved him and honored him all these years.

✿ Up at Aunt Hattie's

AFTER MY MOTHER lost her parents, she went to live at Aunt Hattie's. Aunt Hattie was the widow of Mamma's Uncle Ben, and she ran a boarding house, though of course it was almost too refined to be thought of as such. Aunt Hattie had been Miss Harriet Taylor from Fitzwilliam County, and she was from mighty fine folks; that was obvious, Mamma said. She was to the manner born and every inch a lady, but after Uncle Ben died she had to do something to make ends meet (though Aunt Hattie had had "a man among men" carved on his tombstone, he had not been very successful in business). The most genteel thing one could do in those days was to take in boarders, and that is what she did.

I do not know whether she ever charged Mamma rent or not, but it could not have been very much if she did because I once heard somebody say she charged only twenty dollars a month for room and board. Of course that was a great deal for working people (and that is what Aunt Hattie's boarders were—clerks downtown or school teachers) to pay back in 1917. Mamma had gone to work almost right after her parents died, though I do not think she really had to. She went to work for Dr. Hubbard, the dentist, and to the end of her life, gave the impression that she knew more about dentistry than all the American Dental Association put together. Anyhow it was good of Aunt Hattie to "take her in," as they say, and her house did become something of a home for Mamma.

To the end of her days Mamma always expressed doubts (to put it mildly) about Aunt Hattie's methods of running a boarding house, no matter how good and motherly Aunt Hattie had been to her. In the first place, Mamma said, Aunt Hattie was not herself *about* to cook (and that was always the worst thing, short of a real moral lapse, that Mamma could say about any woman any time—that she would not cook). She did not even get the best Negro cook she could find, she just put up with old Aunt Mag who was too old and ailing half the time really to care what or how she cooked. A lot of the time they had canned vegetables to eat even though there were plenty of fresh ones right in the market or growing in folks' own gardens. Aunt Hattie was not about to mess around with that—not that she thought gardening was beneath her, being a Taylor from Fitzwilliam County and all; she just did not want to take the time and effort to fool with it. She had much rather sit in the living room and talk to her "guests," as she more or less treated her boarders, or else she would take her seat at the dinner table and visit with each one as he came in to eat at noon and not get up until the last one had gone back to town, work, or wherever he belonged. Mamma said Aunt Hattie could act the hostess better than most any woman she had ever seen but that she was not long on elbow grease.

When there was not enough going on at home to interest her, Aunt Hattie would call on the neighbors (Aunt Mag and Beauty, the maid, did all the real housework), or else she would go to a funeral. Aunt Hattie was a great funeral-goer; sometimes she took Beauty with her to have somebody to lean on after she wrenched her back. To everybody in town the sight of a tall stout woman all in black (which she wore all her life after Uncle Ben died) leaning on the arm of a short, dumpy colored woman, meant Aunt Hattie and Beauty were coming back from a funeral. (Nobody ever seemed to remark on their going to a funeral; it was just the coming back they noticed.) Aunt Hattie loved to travel, too. With her limited means and her living to make, she naturally could not get too far from home; mainly she visited in Fitzwilliam County. But one time she did get as far away as Chicago, to go to a national meeting of the WCTU, of which she was a powerful big member; she always wore the white ribbon and all that. I do not know what, if anything, she had against liquor. None of her folks ever drank that I know of, and neither did Uncle Ben's, but it was the right thing to be against back then, I suppose. She was no battle-axe, Carrie Nation-type of saloon-smasher-up either. It was all a good moral cause—like religion—to her and ranked, I gather, along with the purity of womanhood and the sanctity of the married state in her mind.

O, I think she would pass a little pitcher of whiskey to go in the boiled custard at Christmastime. She was certainly no dried up old kill-joy, but that was as far as she ever went, I am sure. And I do not suppose she ever told or heard an improper joke in her life. In fact, Mamma said one time that Aunt Hattie was probably so pure that she did not recognize that ladies had legs: their shoes were just pinned to the bottom of their dresses! There was the famous tale about the time when they all got ready to hang up their stockings the Christmas after Mamma moved up there. (I suppose they never really meant to but were having fun talking about it.) Daddy and Uncle Buford, who were both boarding at Aunt Hattie's then, got tickled and said that, if Aunt Hattie ever hung up her stocking, it would take a Majestic range to fill it up because she was on the hefty side, though of course nobody would ever say anything to her like that. The mere thought of such an indelicacy would make one blush, Mamma said, to say nothing of what it would have done to Aunt Hattie.

Of course this is all leading up to the main thing I know about Aunt Hattie's boarding house: it was where Mamma and Daddy really got to know each other and where they really started courting. Somebody who had known them both back in the old days even joked to me when I was a teenager that my parents had lived together before they were married. I was a little discomfited because of the normal "sensitive" feelings of that age, I suppose, but Mamma thought it was very funny and not indelicate at all. But then she was cut from a different piece of cloth than Aunt Hattie, or even from Daddy, for that matter. (He was inclined to be prudish, despite the fact that he was a big talker and a bold one; Mamma was never that way.)

In later years, when Mamma and Daddy would get together with some of their other chums who had lived at Aunt Hattie's in the old days, they would laugh and giggle about all the fun they had had there and really act like they were more or less graduates of the same school, talking over old times on campus. They would recollect the time when some visiting milliner (there used to be traveling milliners in those days who would go from town to town showing their wares at the local dry good stores) had referred to having stayed for a whole week over in "that God-forsaken Fitzwilliam County." Aunt Hattie swelled up liked a stuffed toad frog; but she could not say anything because, after all, the milliner was a "guest" in her home.

Then there was the time that Uncle Buford was home from the Navy in World War I and came to stay with Daddy at Aunt Hattie's and he let it out that sometimes he walked in his sleep (which was the truth). All the ladies living there went to tee-heeing about getting keys for their doors and locking themselves in at night and who knows what all. There was a lot of put-on alarm and embarrassment for all concerned. As a matter of fact, Uncle Buford always said that, when he walked in his sleep, he knew perfectly well what he was doing and, if somebody would simply call his name, he would wake right away and be all right. Of course they made a little drama out of his condition at Aunt Hattie's.

Daddy was working for Mr. Randolph then, in his hardware store, and he was a very much trusted employee—a very valuable one, I gather. One time Mr. Randolph sent Daddy to a Winchester Repeating Arms convention up in New Haven, Connecticut. These meetings were held at Yale, and right now I have a photograph of Daddy and several other Tennesseans posed together outside Woolsey Hall, where, years later, I was to hear many a concert and lecture when I went to graduate school at Yale. This was in 1920, before Daddy and Uncle Buford were in business for themselves as Drake Brothers, and it was a great thing for anybody from our town to go to Connecticut, much less attend meetings on the Yale campus. (I think they even went to a game in the Yale Bowl but am not certain about that.)

All this time Mamma was working for Dr. Hubbard, the dentist, and she and Daddy were thrown together every day. But at that stage Mamma's whole life did not center around living at Aunt Hattie's or even around Daddy. She was too busy watching and helping with all the "interesting" inlay work Dr. Hubbard was doing. Right across the hall from his office was the office of Watson and Watson, the big lawyers that everybody always got to sue people for them—or to defend them in case they were being sued themselves. There was also the office of Dr. William Harris whom Mamma had known all her life as she had known Ezra Watson in the Watson and Watson firm. And they were always catching her in the hall and telling her about some of the more bizarre things they had had to deal with in their respective practices.

I do not know whether it was all strictly ethical, but I gather they felt they could trust Mamma because they had known her all their lives. Mamma was certainly a lively talker but not a notorious one. She always said to me, "You never hear me quoted around town as saying this or that." And it was the truth too. Of course, Mary Belle Johnson, that had also grown up with Mamma, was trying hard back then to catch Dr. Harris, but Mamma did not think much of that and, apparently, neither did he because he told Mamma he could not even afford to buy Mary Belle's clothes. (Her father was a banker, and she always was well dressed). And then Ezra Watson was always getting Mamma to witness wills when people signed them; she explained to me that it really was not very exciting because you did not have to know what was in the will to witness it. Ezra did tell Mamma about one of his clients who was suing her husband for a divorce because he was keeping a colored woman, by whom he had had a child, on the side. That was a very much bated-breath thing to tell back in those days, but, as I say, they had all grown up together and therefore trusted Mamma. She certainly never told any of this promiscuously—only spoke of it to Daddy and me, and that was years later. Mamma loved being downtown, I think; it was not just the money her job brought her. Later, after I was born, Daddy said she loved to be in the thick of things so much that it was a wonder she did not take an apartment over one of the store buildings down on the square.

Anyhow, all of this time Daddy was working for Mr. Randolph and saving his money. Really, I think he always hoped Mr. Randolph would take him into the business as a partner some day, but he never did. A few years later, Uncle Buford, who had also been working for Mr. Randolph, went down to Memphis and took a bookkeeping course. Then he and Daddy opened up Drake Brothers; Daddy furnished the capital out of his savings, and Uncle Buford supplied the skill he had acquired with finances. They stayed in business together until Daddy's death thirty-five years later, and as far as I

The Drake Brothers store, pictured here shortly after it opened in 1921, sold grocery staples and hardware.

know, there was never a cross word between them. Uncle Buford was the apple of Daddy's eye (he was seven years younger than Daddy), and I think Daddy always thought of him as a little boy who needed looking after. I know that when I was growing up—even after I was in college—Daddy would call me "Buford" half the time. It used to make me angry until I understood more the nature of the bond between them. Uncle Buford was not as demonstrative or outwardly affectionate as Daddy, but I could tell how much he thought of him all the same. I never saw him shed a tear until the day Daddy died, and then it was all over in a minute, as if he had gotten it out of his system and was ready to go on to whatever he had to do at such a time. Uncle Buford could grieve all right, but he was practical about everything else, and there was no point in crying when there were things that had to be done, practical matters that had to be looked after.

All these years, at Aunt Hattie's, Mamma and Daddy were together every day and every night. I do not know exactly when they began thinking seriously about each other or whether there was ever

any one moment when they fell in love, but I suspect it happened as
a result of propinquity and their getting used to each other and
having an enormous respect for each other's characters or something
like that. Because in many ways, they were very different. As I have
said, Daddy was a big, bold talker, but Mamma was more delicate,
even sly, in her conversation. They did make a good pair: that was
obvious. Both of them were highly strung, as we used to say, though
Mamma usually concealed her temperament more than Daddy.
Anything could make Daddy's eyes fill with tears—anything sweet
or sentimental like Mother's Day or a new baby in the neighborhood. Mamma was not as outwardly affected; she took things more
to heart, for good or for bad, than he did, and she never forgot a
kindness, or an unkindness, either. They must have seemed to their
friends a well-matched pair. Both of them had been engaged—or
nearly so—before; thus they were not coming to each other in the
first fine flush of romance. From the moment they decided to marry,
I do not think either one of them ever had doubts or second thoughts
about it; they were warmly affectionate all their lives—Daddy sometimes treating Mamma like a little girl who needed a father, she
sometimes treating him like a little boy who needed mothering.
Whatever else their relationship was, it was warm and deep. The
only thing that could have made either one of them think of anything
else was my birth, and that did not really change anything; it only
made their relationship deeper and more lasting, or so it seems to
me. Certainly, I never came between them in any way: neither one
was ever jealous of me. After all, I was the product of their love for
each other, a deeper and different relationship from anything they
might have felt toward me separately, and I belonged to them both.

They must have courted for three or four years; they never said
much about those times, only about the fun they had when they
were all living together at Aunt Hattie's. Were they too shy to
mention such things around me? Of course, like many people my
age, I never received any sexual instruction at home, and, despite
the warmth of their devotion to each other, I did not think of my
parents as in any way sexual creatures until I was almost grown.
Daddy would observe that he had courted Mamma under Aunt
Hattie's own dignified eye and that that had been pretty difficult but

that Mamma did not have anywhere else to turn and that was why he
had caught her. Then she would bridle up and say that indeed she
could have if she had wanted to: what about Mr. Jamieson who was a
graduate of Chapel Hill and had courted her so long until she turned
him down? Daddy would say that Mr. Jamieson was nothing but a
jack-leg Methodist preacher that could never have made a living for
Mamma, and she would say anybody that had gotten through both
Chapel Hill and the Vanderbilt Divinity School could do anything
he pretty much wanted to and, besides, any fool could make money.
Daddy would then die laughing because he said Mamma was always
too feisty for him and that she and Mr. Jamieson could never have
produced me. That always seemed to settle everything for both
of them.

They were married in Aunt Hattie's living room by Brother
Cleanth Brooks, who was their beloved Methodist pastor and whose
son later became one of the best friends I ever had when he was my
mentor at Yale (how strange is life, with what impossible coinci-
dences!). Brother Brooks was supposed to have baptized me, they
always told me, but that was impossible because by the time I
arrived on the scene he and his family had moved to another church
in Louisiana. I gather the wedding was a very quiet affair, with only
Uncle Buford, Aunt Hattie, and Mamma's old-maid cousins on
hand, with of course Aunt Mag and the faithful Beauty peering
around the dining room door. Then they took the night train for
Memphis and their honeymoon. The local newspaper account of
their marriage was very eloquent, after the fashion of the times. It
began by saying that the union came as a surprise to the couple's
wide circle of friends and that they had really "stolen a march on the
old folks." It went on to describe the groom as a "fine, upstanding"
leader of the local business community and the bride as "extremely
popular" among the younger set.

Not long afterwards Aunt Hattie decided to close her boarding
house and go to live with a recently widowed sister in Fitzwilliam
County, but she always came back to see Mamma and Daddy from
time to time. When I was a little boy, I remember how she loved to
eat and talk at the same time. (Mamma said the main thing was that
Aunt Hattie would not take the trouble to cook for herself, so she

never really got enough to eat until she went visiting, and then she would lay back her ears and go to it.) When you asked her what else she wanted at the table, she would say, "Just time, honey, just time." That meant more time to eat and talk, I suppose. Whenever she came, Mamma and Daddy were always glad to see her. They would sit around the table and talk over the old times when they were all living at her house with so much relish that I often felt left out. I knew that it was something that they all had among them that I could never participate in, much less really understand, and perhaps I was a little inclined to resent that. As I grew older, I began to see that, though I could not share this experience with them, some day I would have my own Aunt Hatties (my school? my college? my office?) to talk about, and that was all that really mattered.

❧ *Down in the Bottom*

IN THE FIRST PLACE, the Drakes said not a one of them had ever lost a thing down in the Mississippi Bottom, which was about ten or twelve miles west of Woodville and Maple Grove. Aside from the natural inconveniences of the place, the folks down there were not like other folks: they all lived high, wide, and handsome, mostly on credit until the cotton crop came in—if it came in—and paid for it later if at all. That was no way to do, according to the Drakes, who did not want to be obligated to any man, no matter what kind of expectations they might have for the future. Daddy said there were but two classes of people down in the Bottom—millionaires and sharecroppers. (Negroes did not count because they were always the same more or less wherever they lived.) That was no healthy state of affairs for white folks or anybody else either.

My mother, I think, took a somewhat different view, one reason being that her first cousin, Billy Moss, whom she loved dearly, had married Miss Effie Boyd, from down in the Bottom at Boyd's Landing, which was right on the river. Mamma used to go to Cousin Effie's, before she married Cousin Billy, to big house parties that Cousin Effie's folks always were giving; there would be guests there from as far away as Memphis and Nashville all jammed into the Boyds' big old white house that had porches running all around it both downstairs and upstairs so that it looked like a steamboat. The Boyds lived high on the hog, depending on how good a crop they had made the year before. But, no matter what, there were always enough Negroes all over the place to do all the work and wait on everybody, so everything was fairly painless as far as the Boyds were concerned. No matter how much cash they actually had on hand

Open Lake today. Photo by Michael O'Brien.

right then, it sure looked grand. Old Mr. Boyd, Cousin Effie's father, had a general store where he sold everything from plow-shares to coffins (mostly, though, he raised hundreds of acres of cotton). He sold whiskey, too—all perfectly legal even if the county was dry because he would put prospective customers on a boat and run them out into the middle of the river and sell it to them there, where neither Tennessee nor Arkansas had any jurisdiction. This stratagem was called "making the loop," and my mother always spoke of it with glee as one more happy memory of the good old times.

Mamma had also always enjoyed camping, along with Cousin Effie's folks, at Open Lake, which was about five miles back from the river but was fed by its waters. Some high old times were had there by the men who hunted and fished and by the women who mostly talked and played cards. In those days, there were no camp houses down at the lake; they merely pitched three tents for every group— one for the men, one for the women, and a third for the Negro cooks, where everyone ate their meals. Never were such good times had anywhere, according to Mamma—the fishing and the hunting, the card-playing, the eating, and, above all, the talking. When I used to ask her what they talked about, she would say, "O, anything and everything." I imagine now that a lot of it was "man talk" and "girl talk," carefully segregated in those days of course, about, on the one hand, conquests of both game and girls and, on the other, gossip of flirtations and pending engagements or perhaps breakups. None of them was married in those days at the lake, but of course they were always suitably chaperoned by Cousin Effie's parents and other dowagers and patriarchs. After marriage the lake somehow did not seem to hold its allure for them, but they all—Mamma, Cousin Effie, and the rest—liked to talk about it still. The lake did not lend itself to domesticity: you could not imagine anybody ever living there in the married state.

Did they think that the lake—and the whole Bottom, for that matter—was a kind of fine playground suitable for flirting and fun but not really appropriate to live one's whole life in? Did they think it was all a region where standards of conduct were momentarily relaxed and the time given over to courtship and frolic but never a possibility as far as three-hot-meals-a-day living was concerned? Of course, it was fun to have been there, but who would ever want to live there, except for people like Cousin Effie and her family? And look what it did to them.

I realize now that I am speaking more for the Drakes than for anybody else here because that was certainly their view of every-thing that either went on down in the Bottom or else came out of it. No good, certainly, could come of all that card-playing (the Drakes never had a "spot" card in the house), to say nothing of the drinking (the Drakes would put a little spiking in the boiled custard at Christmastime but that was all). And, with manners so free and easy, who could expect much from their morals?

I do not mean to make the Drakes sound like old dried-up prigs here; nobody loved real fun more than they did. But their fun was without benefit of appurtenances or auxiliaries; with their back-ground and their orientation, to say nothing of their means, which were certainly limited, they were used to making their own fun, not importing it. They viewed all such other ways of life with a somewhat jaundiced eye. I do not think that my mother ever went so far as that: her background was somewhat more free-wheeling and high-stepping than that of the Drakes. But she would observe from time to time that there certainly was no other family on earth like the Boyd family and that maybe some people would have been a whole lot better off if they never had seen that Bottom.

Here I always imagined she was thinking of Cousin Billy, who married Cousin Effie, because Mamma did not seem to think, for all that she loved Cousin Effie, that his association with the Boyds had done him any particular good. They certainly seemed to encourage his drinking and gambling, or else they turned a blind eye to them. Although Mamma was more "liberal" than the Drakes, she could not ignore that. The main thing, according to Mamma, was that the Boyds were such a contentious family. For all that they seemed to love each other, they could never resist an argument about anything: men, women, dogs, even the time of the day. Mamma said that, if necessary with no one else around, a Boyd could even argue with himself. Of course Daddy could never see how anybody could quarrel with his own folks, but then I do not think he ever understood what lay behind the Boyds' perpetual arguing: for them, no animus was involved, only principle. The principle, which they never stated, seemed mainly to be concerned with who could get the better of whom, and how—what today we would probably call one-upmanship. The Drakes did not feel that they had to prove anything to anybody, certainly not to themselves, and they did not believe in gilding the lily about anything.

Cousin Effie's oldest sister, Miss Leona, was a Mrs. Hamilton, but her husband never did amount to much so she devoted all her time (she never had any children) to telling Cousin Effie and all her other brothers and sisters what to do. Mamma said Mrs. Hamilton was a born *dictator* and lazy, too: whatever happened, Mamma said, Mrs. Hamilton would *not* cook. Mainly she spent her time seated in a big rocking chair in the middle of the living room floor playing solitaire (she had a big board made to lay across her arm chair for that purpose), telling everybody else what to do. Well, when one day Mrs. Hamilton felt called on to observe to Daddy about somebody's untimely death that she well knew what it was like to experience such a tragedy because her brother Paul had died so young himself, Daddy snorted, when he was safely home, that indeed he did remember Brother Paul's untimely death: he was shot dead in a crap game by a Negro (who was subsequently not lynched but given only a light sentence in the state pententiary) on the Fourth of July about thirty years before. And if anybody ever deserved to get shot, he said, it was Brother Paul, who was so feisty and obnoxious that everyone knew he was born to be hung or shot, whichever came first.

Anyhow, that was what the Bottom represented to the Drakes—a place where the usual rules did not apply, even occasionally a place for downright outlawry, like in the case of Jim Bob Thomas who ran what was euphemistically called the Boyd's Landing Hotel but was nothing but a cover for an extensive bootlegging and prostitution operation. Daddy said the Lord only knew how many men had gone down in the Bottom to see Jim Bob Thomas on "business" and never returned to tell the tale. One time he even slit a woman's throat from ear to ear (one of his "girls"?) and God knows what else. The tales about him were indeed legion (he was supposed to hide his whiskey from the revenue agents by nailing it up in the wall!). I had heard so much about him that when I finally did see him (one day down at the courthouse) it was all an anticlimax. He was so meek and mild looking that he could have passed for a Sunday school superintendent, which, I suppose, is one more instance where truth is stranger than fiction.

But of all the outlaws in the Bottom, the river itself was the biggest because you never knew what it was going to do—make you as rich as Croesus because it left behind a fertile deposit on your land when it rose, or else wipe you out completely if there was a big enough flood. Who in the world wanted to live the kind of existence that called for building your house on stilts and your barn on an artificial mound of earth (so the stock could climb up out of the high water to safety)? It was enough to be at the mercy of the other elements without taking on the river. One good thing could be said about it, according to Daddy: every drop of water that fell in Nashville, Knoxville, St. Louis, or Cincinnati sooner or later had to come by Boyd's Landing. It gave him pleasure to think that our county was so close to the lifeline of the country, to say nothing of its oldest highway. Our county just could not be beat, he said.

The time Cousin Effie broke her leg summed it all up for him. She and Cousin Billy were living at Boyd's Landing in a house the Boyds had built for them which Daddy said was a mistake in the first place: Cousin Billy ought to have known better than to take anything from them. Anyway, Cousin Effie fell down the back steps and broke her leg, but they could not get to Woodville because the high water was up. They did the next best thing and put her on a boat and went across to Luxora, Arkansas, where they put her on the train for Memphis. Like all stretcher cases in those days, she rode in the baggage car, but this time there were armed guards riding there because of recent holdups along the line (and this was no longer ago than 1917 though it sounds like the Old West).

They finally got her to Memphis and took her right away to the Baptist Hospital, where Dr. Henry Boyd, who was her cousin and a

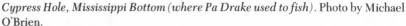

Cypress Hole, Mississippi Bottom (where Pa Drake used to fish). Photo by Michael O'Brien.

leading bone doctor, was going to operate on her. They got her in the operating room, and she was not much afraid since it was her own cousin who was going to do the operating. But as she was looking among the white-robed figures to find him and perhaps have a word with him before they "put her under," all of a sudden a deep bass voice from behind her said, "Do you have anything you wish to say before I administer the anesthetic?" That like to have scared her to death—as if they were asking for her famous last words before springing the trap or throwing the switch—and she practically fainted right there, just to oblige everybody. The next thing she knew she was waking up with a silver nail in her leg that she carried there until the day she died. I thought it all a very exciting tale and used to love to hear Cousin Effie tell it over and over when I was little. (I loved to hear her tell about Christmastime—"Tell me a Christmas," I would beg her—on their place in the old days, too. For instance, once Santa Claus filled one stocking so full that it fell into the churn which had been put in front of the fire for the milk to turn and ruined everything in it.) Daddy said it all went to show what came of living down in the Bottom: you could have it all in silver or gold, with lots of Negroes to do the work, but sooner or later you still had to face up to what and how you were going to pay the piper. That was the one thing you could always count on, no matter who you were or where you lived.

❧ Daddy the Talker, Daddy the Lover

MY FATHER ALWAYS SAID you could take a deaf-mute and make a barber out of him and he would be talking in six months. I suppose that is the truth because I have never seen a barber yet that could not talk you to death and then bend down and whisper in your ear afterwards. I suppose it goes with the profession. For one thing, barbers do have a captive audience: once they have you all tucked into that big apron and safely ensconced in that big chair, you are caught and unable very well to do anything but listen for the next twenty minutes or however long they take. I have even found that language is no particular barrier. Once, when I was in Seville on a tour through Andalusia, I was having my hair cut, and, though I spoke no Spanish and the barber certainly was not up to English, he favored me, after appropriate nods and becks and wreathed smiles, with a couple of arias from *The Barber of Seville* and thus communicated with me though not directly head-on, as it were.

Daddy himself was one of the world's biggest talkers in a family none of whom was noted for pregnant—or even barren—silences. Once when he became exasperated with my own flow of speech, he turned to Uncle Buford and demanded, "I've never heard such a talker. Wherever does the boy get it from?" Uncle Buford looked him square in the eye and said, "Right there," not fazing Daddy, who would always say my talking came from Mamma's side of the house—meaning the Woods. But Mamma's family were all desultory talkers: back and forth and up and down. Their speech was all measured and mannered, not the non-stop flow of words that came rolling out of the Drakes, but then I must not do them an injustice either: what the Drakes had to say was never dull, none of them was ever a bore. They seemed, rather, as if they might be afraid of silence and had to have some sort of sound to fill up the void. And so they talked—about politics, the weather, the ones in the family that were dead and gone, the old times at Maple Grove; but never was there any idle or malicious gossip and never anything remotely off-color (though all five brothers liked a good story).

Daddy loved to take the floor (not to dominate, but to perform) and tell a tale, and he knew well that he was a good talker, that people loved to hear him, and that he never bored anybody. (He also knew when to listen, too, and I think that is important. All good talkers are good listeners; that is the way they perfect and refine their own art. On the other hand, bores never listen to anybody: that is why they are bores.) Daddy would light one of his big cigars (he favored the "Flor de Melba," which was named after the opera star, Nellie Melba, and the brand had a picture of her on the inside of the box) and use it like a baton to punctuate his talk and also to command the attention and involvement of his listeners. If he was feeling really relaxed and among intimates, he would pull up a coal scuttle beside him to have something to spit in and lean back in his rocking chair and, between his strong puffs of smoke, really launch forth, on out into the emptiness that he was artfully populating with characters, their deeds, their shape and form.

In this guise, he could be particularly effective, if not nerve-racking, when we were preparing to go out for some function which required us to be dressed up and properly outfitted for an occasion. He would make his own preparations early and then draw his big rocker (the one that had belonged to Pa) out into the middle of the floor (from where he could direct traffic, Mamma said), then, with the coal scuttle beside him, comment on our lack of haste and the probability that we would all be late for whatever we were going to and why in the world were we going anyhow. Everybody knew *he* did not like to get all dressed up like a country corpse, as he put it, and go out into what people called "society." He would then take a huge puff on his cigar of the moment and spit emphatically and decisively into the coal scuttle, as if to say that he had made himself heard, no matter what the final outcome, and that he was not responsible anymore.

My mother, of course, never turned a hair and went on as deliberately as ever with her preparations. She never hurried, always took her time, never got in a sweat about anything, and always managed to get where she was going on time. I think this seeming lack of haste annoyed Daddy. If something was important, then why not act like it and give the appearance of being all caught up and wrought up in it? That is the way he acted, certainly, but not her. One thing that particularly annoyed him was her fondness for visiting with her friends over the telephone. She did not drive and in later years arthritis prevented her walking long distances. It was nothing for her to talk to one of her friends for an hour, even two hours, over the telephone some nights after supper and before bedtime. Her greatest telephone friend was another lady about her age named Hilda Warren. One night after supper Daddy went to town for the forty-two game (about which I will say more later) and left Mamma talking to Hilda and when he came back she was still talking to her.

Daddy of course had no use for telephones; he looked on them as a mere convenience, used them rarely and briefly, and his manner then was brusque and peremptory. He never lowered his voice at such times either, and I used to ask him why he did not just stick his head out the window and holler: they would hear him as well that way as over the phone. Of course, that always riled him and he would start in on the Woods and their telephone-talking and say I was going to take after them if I did not watch out. I suppose, to some extent, I did because when I was in high school one of my good buddies, a girl named Sally Ann Lightfoot, and I nearly always used to translate our Latin and work our algebra over the telephone. We had many calls back and forth every night and so on, and it is a wonder our parents put up with it. Still, I suppose they thought it was keeping us out of mischief and using the telephone was a harmless enough inconvenience if not a regular vice.

I think what it all came down to was that Daddy, without being conscious of it, wanted a live audience and he wanted it there all around him because essentially he was a performer. Like a regular actor, he wanted to perform to a good house, and he wanted a working rapport with his group and some immediate sense of how it all was going. O, of course, you could say he was a show-off, and perhaps some people may have thought that he was. But really he was not. He gave value received, and he never hogged the floor. After he had told his tale or tales, he was through and would then sit back and listen. (Remember what I said earlier about all good talkers being good listeners; he was certainly one.)

Of course, he did enjoy the audience's reaction to what he had to say, and he occasionally could be egged on by them. I remember one time when my mother and I wanted to go to a grand wedding at the Baptist Church; we made him get all dressed up and go with us, and he was determined not to have a good time and to let how he felt be known publicly, too. It happened that we were seated in one of the Sunday school rooms, whose folding doors had been opened into the auditorium because it was a big wedding, and a lot of our friends were there. As Daddy put it later, he "showed out" by commenting in a stage whisper on all the family and special guests who were being escorted to their seats marked with white ribbons and also on the wedding party itself when it entered. "This is a 200-pound wedding; I can certainly see that," he observed, and, to tell the truth, all the bridesmaids were on the hefty side. But I was about fourteen then and dreadfully embarrassed by the whole thing, and I could have died because all the friends around us were having a field day (had they not wanted to come to the wedding either?) and continually were egging Daddy on—not that he needed urging, for he was a real performer. At the time, it was all a great mortification.

Of course, where Daddy really shone in conversation was in Drake Brothers store. He knew everybody that came into the store, and that, sooner or later, meant about everybody in the county. He was prepared to listen to everything they had to say and then talk to them in turn, and wherever there was laughing and talking and teasing and joking, he was sure to be right in the middle of it all. But as I said earlier, I never heard him tell an off-color story, and he had no taste for such matters either. That came as a big surprise to a lot of people; because he was a big and bold talker, they naturally assumed he would welcome such stories.

I hardly ever heard him use profanity and never did he utter an obscenity. He made himself known all right, however, and no mistake. I remember one time he stopped on the square to admire a new baby, a little girl who had been born to some friends of ours "late in life," as they say. Daddy, after having pronounced all well with the child, turned to the mother and said, "Now you'll have to give her a little brother." She replied, "O, no, I can't cut the mustard any more," and it embarrassed Daddy to death. He said, "She ought not to have talked that way to me." It was useless for me to point out that he had made himself liable for such a rejoinder by his own remarks. To him, that was only teasing; he had not meant to be taken seriously and anybody that knew him ought to have realized that.

That is what Daddy was finally—a first-rate tease. All the Drakes were, and indeed some people thought they went too far. One of my aunts said she thought they all really had a perverted sense of humor: they laughed when people fell down, ran into chairs in the dark, or in any way made fools of themselves in public. But they were all highly selective, for they laughed always at the pompous, the vain, the frivolous, never at the meek, the unfortunate, or the downtrodden. They could be serious too; all that Methodist background had not been wasted on them. Uncle John, the oldest brother, who was a Methodist preacher, could laugh with the best of them, though; he said the funniest thing he ever saw in his life was a man getting a tooth pulled. He liked wrestling matches, too, which Mamma said were not very "uplifting" for a preacher. Anyhow, Daddy was a tease from the word *go*, and his teasing did not stop short with the young or the middle-aged either. He would come down on the old if he thought they deserved it and needed it, like saying to some old man known to be of a miserly nature, "What're you going to do with all that money? You know, they don't make shrouds with pockets in them." Then when somebody with a lot of money died and the question would come up of how much he had left, Daddy would look very knowing and nod his head and say, "He left it *all*." That would settle that.

But I think even then, when I was growing up, I was aware that behind the teasing, behind all the talk, lay something richer and deeper. One minute Daddy would take my head, as he held me firmly between his legs, and turn it abruptly to the right, then to the left, then back to its center position while intoning: "Look thisaway. Look thataway. See nobody coming? Dig! Dig! Dig!" Then he would nod my head up and down three times on that last line as though to make me agree with him, no matter what he had observed or proposed. I would be tickled but halfway outraged too. Or he would bounce me on his knee and chant out an old counting-out rhyme like

One saw
Two saw
Little Dicky Dan.
Bob-tail
Dominecker
Deal Doy Dan.
Isaac, Aaron
Virgin Mary.
Harum, scarum
Zingum
Zangum
Bolum, buck.

Then, on the last word, he would catch me to him and hug me hard and root around on my stomach with his day-old beard that tickled me and make snorting noises as though he really, as he said, loved me so much that he was going to eat me up.

Because I knew then, even as I know now, that his love for me was absolutely without qualification; he did not love me because I was smart or good or anything else, not even finally because I was his. He loved me because I was myself—the way I always imagined that God, if He really was not going to "get" me as I had often inferred from the Bible, might love me. All the talk, all the teasing were not covers-up for such a tender heart and so much love; they were also expressions of it. You do not talk to people, do not tease people you care nothing about. It took me a long time to learn that; I was almost grown, but I suppose I could not have learned it any sooner. But I am awfully glad I learned it before Daddy died—learned then how much he really did love me and Mamma and almost everybody else (he said he never had hated anybody in his life but he always knew a fool when he saw one). Now, after all these years, I realize more than ever how great such a gift was—the one he made to me in such love. And I feel it—all his talk, all his love—still blessing me in both tears and laughter every day, every year, a whole lifetime through.

❧ The Little Girl with the Blue Eyes

IN THE PHOTOGRAPH SHE STANDS, a little girl about five years old, clutching her doll in one hand and her cat in the other. Her dark hair explodes into ringlets, naturally curly, and she is dressed in what looks like her Sunday best: a long dress, full-skirted, almost touching the ground, with puffed sleeves and lots of rick-rack for trimming. It is difficult to know precisely of course because the original picture was old and faded, but many years ago I took it to a photographic studio to be "restored" and that is what emerged from the old print. I told the young woman who waited on me at the studio not to dress up the photograph, only to restore it, in color, so that it would be clear and fresh, and this was the result. Her dress is red, her cat is gray, and her eyes are blue, the latter being the only thing I could be sure of—always the blue eyes. The other colors were guesses, and the studio did not demur, but the eyes were blue. I was firm about that. She was my mother, and always people—both within and outside the family—remembered her eyes, for they were the brightest blue one could imagine, almost like cornflowers. And in the photograph they are dazzling, as winning and loving as ever. One of the cousins even used to call her "Miss Blue Eyes," but of course her name was Lillian.

I never could make up my mind about the name Lillian. It was not what I would have called a tacky name like Viola or a comfortable name like Bessie, and it was not elegant like Elizabeth. It had probably been fashionable back when people were reading Tennyson all over the place because it sounded far-off and romantic. At least it was better than Vivien or Elaine, but it was dated by the time I came along.

94

Clutching a doll, the author's mother stands, around 1894, with her family in front of her childhood home.

The photograph is something I have always cherished. For one thing, it had been taken by Uncle John, and he said he had always considered that photograph of my mother one of his masterpieces. I never knew exactly why. It was taken years before anybody ever thought of her marrying into the Drake family. The fact that my mother and father had many relatives in common but were not actually kin themselves always used to fascinate me for some reason. The concept of *kinfolks* was almost a mystique in that world where I grew up some forty years ago in the rural South, and I know the word always had some special distin.ction for me: it described a strange and baffling mystery which was all a part of your own self, your background, your past. Like it or not, there was nothing you could do about it. One old soul of our acquaintance even observed that God gave you kinfolks but, thank the Lord, you could choose your friends.

The idea that my mother had once been a little girl four or five years old standing there with her dolly and her kitty to have her picture taken was fascinating, if somewhat incomprehensible, to me when I first saw the photograph as a child. I was a child, and she was my mother. Between us there yawned a vast and unbridgeable tract of years. It was hard to think of her as ever being a child, loving, needing to be loved, with her blue eyes, which were still so distinctive, looking toward the outside world with something like both delight and fear. But she had been a little girl, and my father, when he was especially pleased or amused with something she had said or done, would always shake his head in delight and say, "Mamma's just like a little girl, so full of laughter and mischief."

I knew that my parents never called each other by their Christian names: she was always "Mamma" at home or, to outsiders, "Miss Lillian," and he was always "Daddy" or "Jucks," which was his nickname. I think she had, when they first married, tried calling him by his Christian name, which was the same as my own, but hardly anyone else in the world did that, and she finally gave up. Could they not bear to see themselves, as they were, in their grown-up bodies and natures? Did they have to have the protective covering of other names, names which suggested that somehow they were playing at adulthood and family life? I will never know, I suppose. Certainly, in that time and place, there were many couples who shrank from the open intimacy of first names: my Aunt Estelle bore Uncle John three children and still, after fifty years of marriage, called him "Mr. Drake."

I think always that Daddy preferred to think of Mamma as the little girl—maybe even the little girl with the kitty and the dolly— that he could both pet and spoil. Because she never learned to drive, he was always there to drive her. He and my Uncle Buford were their own masters at their store, and she could therefore call him to come home at any time of the day if she felt lonesome or blue. He was always there to run errands for her, to do whatever she asked.

That was the other side of the coin from the little girl in the photograph: she was still a little girl and needed very much to be loved and cherished. But in her dealings with me my mother was anything but the little girl. She was firm and authoritative in all her opinions and judgments, and from them there was no appeal. I knew I could nearly always get around my father, but not her. It was hard to think of my mother as ever being as defenseless in her love, clutching the dolly and the kitty close as if for aid and comfort, as she seemed in that photograph.

I have often thought what a really terrible crisis she had to go through after her parents died—her home broken up, being turned out into the world, more or less on her own, so suddenly, though of course she was grown. I wondered as I was growing up and came to know more and more about her what such an experience had done to her. Something, I felt sure. The little girl in the photograph had had her playhouse destroyed; she had no mother or father, no home, and her kitty and her dolly were useless now. And yet something remained. There were still the blue eyes, and they were as winning and loving, or needing love, as ever. At least that is what I thought must have been the case.

That was one of the reasons, I thought, why my father married her. She had those blue eyes, so full of love and care, but no dolly, no kitty now, and she needed somebody to look after her. He delighted in doing it. He had recently lost his own mother, and thus I think my mother became at once wife and lover and mother to him. I am sure neither of them would ever have thought of it in those terms; probably they would have been scandalized at the idea, but something like this, I think, always lay at the heart of their relationship. Remember, she called him "Daddy," too, and I do not think that was totally for my benefit either. He did become a kind of surrogate father for the real one she had loved and lost. His father and her

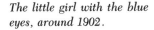

The little girl with the blue eyes, around 1902.

mother ran poor seconds in such matters, though they both seemed
to cherish the greatest affection for them.

They had been married eight years when I was born, and I gather
they had wanted a child badly. They were both middle-aged by
then; she was forty and he was forty-five. When I was growing up
that was a source of discomfort, even shame, to me: all my friends
had young parents that smoked and drank and danced and did God
knows what else, and there I was saddled with what I thought were a
couple of old fogies. I suppose I was ashamed at the thought that I
was the product of old people's passions, of middle-aged lusts. It all
somehow seemed unsuitable, even indelicate. I had no grandparents, except for an ancient paternal grandfather. My parents could
have been my grandparents; they were old enough. Sometimes I
thought they were trying to raise me that way—out-of-date, out-of-
step with the times, as I thought they were. I had to say always "Sir"
and "Ma'am" and of course never use any bald, naked Christian
names to or about other adults. It always had to be "Mr." and
"Miss," which in turn might, if I knew them well enough, be
followed by a Christian name rather than a surname. Always the
ceremonial forms had to be observed.

I suppose it was natural that I should grow up with the past ever
present in my world. It swirled around me continually in the talk of
my parents and their families—particularly my father's—and their
friends; it was always treated as something still very much alive and
highly influential. It never occurred to me then that the past was
over and done with or dead or that anyone might think it was. The
past—and the characters and their actions which made it up—were
realities to my parents and forever present about them, as was the
tradition of talk. And I learned early to keep my mouth shut and my
ears open. How many times was I told that "children should be seen
and not heard" or, as they looked at each other over my head, both
literally and figuratively, that "little pitchers have big ears!" I hated
them for it, while at the same time I longed for the day when I could
enter into their world of adulthood, their world of talk, even their
world of the past. After all, I hardly had any past of my own, and I
would have none until I was grown. Perhaps that would be the
common denominator between me and them then. I both thought

and acted older than I was, to the chagrin of my contemporaries and, I now suspect, the dismay of my parents.

I did grow older in time, and to some extent I was able to come to terms with my parents, if not on a basis of equality, then at least with some concession on their part that I had reached years of discretion and was of age, as they say. But things did not altogether turn out as I had planned. My mother fell ill, some years before my father's death, with what was then termed a nervous breakdown and had to be hospitalized because of her extreme depression (I learned later that it was more or less precipitated by menopause). During this time she grew increasingly dependent on my father and more and more possessive toward me as she wailed that she would be better off dead but that she had no idea of what would happen to us if she were. It was a painful ordeal not only for her but for us, and especially for me, a teenager at the time.

I think I realized then for the first time how perilous, tyrannical, and destructive love could be, for my mother became more and more the little girl with the blue eyes, clutching at both my father and me; she had no dolly or kitty to cling to then. Her eyes were as blue as ever, but they had somehow lost their luster. I know it almost broke my father's heart to see her so miserable, but he stayed behind her through it all and pushed and pulled her back into some degree of health within a year. I did not realize it then—luckily— but this was the first of a series of such illnesses for her. After my father died suddenly when I was at college, she grew worse. She would cry and wring her hands and say again and again, "There's no one to scotch for me anymore, now that Daddy's gone." I both pitied and despised her for her weakness; it was hard for me to think of her condition as an illness. Was she still the little girl with the blue eyes in the photograph, looking tentatively about her, fearful that her love would not be returned by someone, anyone, who might be near? Did she miss the dolly and the kitty even more than ever?

I know that in her last illness, after years of both mental and physical debilitation, she would cling with a surprisingly strong grip to my hand when I would go to sit with her in the hospital, and she would ask me again and again whether I still loved her. I supposed that was better—but not much—than her tears and pleas to be allowed to go home during the previous years when she had been a patient in a state hospital. All the nurses loved her and said how pretty she still was—her hair snow-white but still curly, her eyes as blue as ever if somewhat bleared. I suppose they wondered why I was not more demonstrative and outwardly affectionate. Perhaps I was still afraid of the blue eyes that belonged to the little girl in the photograph with their terrible, defenseless need for love and yet their terrible strength in such weakness. I worried about it considerably but had to play the game all the way out by the rules that I had laid down years before. I would do everything for her I could, but she should not possess, even destroy, me as I suspected she had my father. He was not unwilling, and for that I perhaps unconsciously despised him. It had been his choice, but I accused him in my heart of weakness, I suppose. No, she was not going to take me with her to the grave or into the past or anywhere else. I had my own life to lead, and I had to lead it on my own terms.

A day or two before she died, I arrived at the hospital as the nurses were changing shifts, as I usually managed to do, so that I could talk to both of them about my mother's condition. As we stood there in the sterile gray corridor, I kept asking them how much longer they thought she would linger to suffer what I thought had already been indecently too much; I know I wanted it all over and done with, to end her suffering and (I might as well face facts) also my own. I was not proud of my seeming coldness towards her. At one time it might have been necessary for self-protection but surely not then. Still, the defenseless little girl with the blue eyes and the curly hair preyed on my thoughts. Had she never been loved enough, protected enough, sheltered enough? Was I the one to do it? Had my father been right to try? It was one of those enigmatic puzzles that could never be solved. At any rate, in the midst of my thoughts while talking to the nurses, one of them—the day nurse, I think—said, "You know, a lot of old people, when they come to die, are ready to go, but your mother wants to live. She grips my hand and asks me whether I love her, and of course I do. But it's really only you that she loves. God only knows how much she loves you." I replied that yes, I knew that, and I turned away so they would not see the tears in my eyes at my thoughts, the judgment I was passing on myself.

With all of its perils, had I risked enough to love her properly? Had I been always too afraid of the charm of the blue eyes and the curly hair, the little girl with the dolly and the kitty? Destructive or not, she had loved, she had risked, and she had paid a terrible price for what she had ventured. Had I been rendered incapable of love by such power as was manifested in hers, and whose fault was it anyway? Not altogether hers, I was sure. Had I fought back enough or too much? Had I even tried to love her in return, or had I merely withdrawn into my shell and refused the danger, the opportunity? I was a loser, whichever way I turned, it seemed. It was all a muddle—and a sad one.

I stood there in the hallway pondering it all until the day nurse had collected her things and left; then I joined the other nurse in my mother's room. My mother seemed to be resting comfortably; perhaps she was asleep. But it made no difference. I went over to her bed, took her hand in mine and bent down and whispered, "It's me, Mamma. I'm here."

❧ The Last Old Maid in Town

STRANGELY ENOUGH, I did not realize that my parents were so much older than the parents of my contemporaries until I was well into grammar school. I do remember one time that a friend of his whom I did not particularly like was teasing me about my great affection for my father. I had boasted that my father could do anything, and the man, who must have been about my father's age himself, said, "Why, boy, there're a lot of things your father can't do simply because he's getting old. Why, he's fifty, I'll bet, right now." I was stunned, I remember, and tried to put it all out of my head: my father could not be that old, I thought. The next thing I knew he would be dead, and that was too awful to contemplate.

I suppose I could have done some simple adding and subtracting, but I never did. (Was I afraid of what I might find out?) I did know that Pa was a Confederate veteran. And that must have meant something, but I did not want to think about it. One of my playmates had recently lost her mother, and I was terrified that one or both of my parents might die or be killed in an automobile wreck or something like in newspaper headlines.

These were all things I did not like to dwell on—my parents' ages, their own mortality—anymore than I might have liked then to contemplate my own death. For a number of years I just rocked along, burying my head in the sand and not thinking about any of it. Finally revelation had to come, I suppose, and it came in a rather bizarre way. We were then on the verge of World War II, and everybody had to sign up for ration books—at least all adults did, as I recall. Shortly after my parents had gotten their books, I found them lying somewhere about the house and, out of nothing but idle curiosity, took a look at them. And there were the facts, signed, sealed, and very official. My father was listed as being fifty-five and my mother as fifty. I was ten myself, and I was horrified. They really were that much older! I really was the child of *old* people who probably did not have many years left to them, and all my fears of being orphaned and bereft were not completely idle. From that moment, I began to feel something about myself that might be peculiar or atypical, something that set me apart from my contemporaries.

Before me there yawned vast abysms of time with what horrors I knew not but could only guess. Whatever they might be, I knew there were some things I could count on: seeing my parents get old while I was still young, seeing them die while I was still a child perhaps, being left alone in the world, not belonging to anybody, not really wanted by anybody. It was almost too awful to contemplate. What would I do, where would I go, what would become of me? My parents' own families were all as old or older than they were, so there would be no help from that quarter, and had I not already detected perhaps a note of amusement in my aunts' and uncles' attitudes toward me that somehow I was a freak, an anomaly, an *indulgence* on the part of my parents? Was there not something somehow funny in my very existence. ("I'll never forget the day we heard the news of your father's marriage! None of us had known a thing about it, almost like he was trying to hide it from us. Why, I went in the store that morning and asked for him, and your Uncle Buford, who was holding down the fort, said, 'Why, he's gone to Memphis on his honeymoon!' You could have knocked me over with a feather!")

Then later there was the surprise, even shock, of my birth. ("I'll never forget how excited your father was that morning! He called all of us in the family up and told us he had a football player for a son!") This was always said with a laugh and a knowing aside toward me, the least athletically inclined boy imaginable. (Had I failed my father somehow?) Another old acquaintance told me, in later years, that they had even feared for my mother's safety during delivery at her time of life. ("Why, we were playing bridge that night, just across the street from your house. And we weren't about to leave until you had put in your appearance: we all knew your mother might have a bad time of it. But do you know, we got so engrossed in our bridge game that the doctor came and went, and you had arrived, and we never knew it!") This was always accompanied by much laughter—not unkind—after I was grown and able to assess the facts of the case for myself.

Gradually, as I was growing up, I began to take all this information in and assimilate it as best I could—the stories, the tales of my parents' wedding and early married life, my own birth and early childhood, and I suppose, finally, my principal reaction, at least when I was young, was one of shame: shame that I might have been an afterthought in my parents' lives; shame, on the other hand, that they might have wanted me very badly indeed but had not been able to conceive me until eight years after their marriage; and above all, shame that I was the product of old people's lusts.

I would have given anything for young and glamorous parents, for a pair of "swingers" perhaps, as they might be called today. Not only were their clothes and our house (an old L-shaped affair, where we had to walk through rooms to get to other rooms) tacky, I decided; we did not even have a car. We used the truck that belonged to my father and Uncle Buford's supply store. Everywhere we went, we had to go in that—to Memphis or around town, to visit in the country, no matter where—and everyone could see our shame. Before my time, I think, the store's truck had been painted in the familiar Purina checkerboard pattern, but I was spared that.

None of this seemed to embarrass them, of course—only me. They cared little, apparently, for appearances. They loved nothing better than telling jokes on themselves, especially about their marriage and early married life, things which shamed me inexpressibly because I thought of it all as somehow unsuitable for their place and their years. My mother would tell, with great glee, about how my father had always boasted that when he got married there would be a sign nailed right beside the front door declaring him "boss and manager" of the house. But shortly after they were married, she said, and had moved into their new house (my mother's childhood home that they had remodeled), an old friend who passed by as my father, to help my mother out, was sweeping off the porch, hollered to ask him where his sign was. My father smiled, shook his head, and never said a word. He did little more than that when my mother would tell it on him in later years, but he was usually outspoken, even boisterous, in his opinions, his likes, and dislikes. (Had my mother somehow tamed him? It was somehow shocking to me that either of them might still be capable of such passion.)

Of course, there were jokes at her expense, too, ones she did not mind telling either. One was about their honeymoon, which they had spent at the Gayoso Hotel in Memphis, which I remember as a once elegant hostelry but, in my childhood, on the downgrade, with hideous murals of DeSoto discovering the Mississippi in its lobby, that same lobby that General Forrest had ridden his men into during a lightning raid on Memphis under Federal occupation. Naturally, the thought of my parents' having a honeymoon (like you always saw in the movies and hear about from younger couples) was distasteful to me. Perhaps the sex lives of our parents, or the thought of them, is distasteful to all of us. But again, it all seemed to me that they were too old for such things: *they should have known better*. My mother, for the first and last time in her life, she said, even wore a silk nightgown, the mention of which always made me blush. And what did they do in Memphis anyway, I always wanted to know. They said they went to some shows and ball games and that was about it— nothing really exciting and just as staid as they were.

The funniest thing was what happened to them as they were leaving home for Memphis, right after their marriage. They had been married at my mother's aunt's house and the ceremony had been a quiet and simple one. The only ones present had been some cousins and her aunt and Uncle Buford to "stand up" with them. But it was a gay enough affair for all that, I gather, and afterwards there was a regular concourse of friends to see them off at the station for Memphis on the night train. In those days (1922) of course the train was the only way to travel considerable distances, and I suppose the ceremony had been timed so that they could catch that particular train.

The train arrived, and my parents boarded it. Rice was still dripping from their clothes from where they had been pelted by their friends and well wishers at the station. When the conductor came down the aisle to take their tickets, he observed their situation and remarked, "There seem to be more newlyweds getting on the train at Woodville than any other town on my run. Tell me," he said to my father, "are there any old maids at all left there now?" My father looked him mock-seriously in the eye and said, "No, sir, this was the last one left!"

When my mother got to that part of the story—and it was nearly always she who told it—she would burst into laughter and say, "I should have left him right then." All the listeners would cluck their tongues and smile as though to say that of course they knew she would not have left him for anything in the world and that it was all my father's well-known predisposition for mischief anyhow. Finally, after I had gotten to be a teenager, that tale began to trouble me as though somehow they were trying to hang on to the coquettishness of youth even though by that time both were well stricken in years. I found it tiresome, even annoying to see them still almost flirting with each other under my very nose. Once, when I was in the eighth grade, I think, I heard my mother recount the tale once more to some of the cousins. When she came to the *coda* after the punch line (my father's) and said "I should have left him right then," everyone laughed right on schedule except for me. Then I spoke up rather brightly and said, "Well, if you had, wouldn't I have been in a *mell of a hess*?" More laughter followed, whether at my wit or my boldness I never knew. My mother gave me a look then that I have never forgotten, as though to say she had not realized until then that I was almost grown, at any rate old enough to know about "those things" and also as though, for the first time, she might be seeing me as more than a child, perhaps even a potential adult. For one brief moment there was almost a look of horror in her eyes—something I then did not understand and am not altogether sure that I do now.

Did she wonder then what she and my father had wrought between them? Did she wonder what I, only in my teens, might be thinking of them as adults—not only as parents—what I might have been thinking of their relationship, marital and otherwise, and what I might be thinking of their middle age now verging on old age? The look she gave me was somehow sad. Had I somehow penetrated their private world, their aging romance (and they did still love each other very much, I believe) with my youth, my brashness, my impudence? Had I made her see, if only for a moment, that I thought it all somehow indecorous and unsuitable? Again, I do not know, but I did realize then that I had somehow hurt her in a way I did not altogether understand. And I was sorry.

All the things that I had feared more or less did happen. Both my parents died while I was still comparatively young, and I was left alone with no brothers or sisters, only Uncle Buford, after the older uncles had died, and some first cousins. By that time I had begun to see something of what my older parents had given me, besides the sense of shame that I used to feel. And it was not altogether on one side of the ledger either. Sure, I had a sense of the past, a sense of history from having more or less grown up in the house with it. I knew the county genealogies about as well as anyone else, certainly better than most of my contemporaries. And I knew a great deal, I felt, of the tragedies of old age, of living beyond one's time, of what might be called the cruelties of modern medicine. Perhaps I had experienced *King Lear* before my time. I also had become something of an oracle myself, for I was the one to whom people turned for verification of dates and facts about the past—appropriately, I think, for one with a background such as my own.

There were some things on the positive side too, albeit some of them I would not have sought on my own. There was the sense of apartness, the sense of outsideness that came with being the only child of older parents: I had learned to look and, more important, I had learned to listen. I had been listening to old people talk all my life—their reminiscing, sorrowing, rejoicing, ruminating, it did not matter which, really. And I was outside their world, part of it yet not of it, with a foot in both past and present. More and more, then, my role became that of the observer and, above all, the listener. Set apart from my contemporaries because of my origins, I was set apart from my parents and their families because of the disparity of age. Perhaps I did not belong anywhere, finally. And yet I have come to see that that was not so either, and it explains a lot of things about me perhaps.

It is why I listen as well as look, why I listen as well as talk. It is why I never in my life have felt particularly intimate with anyone. It is why all my life, I have felt alone—not necessarily lonely, just alone. But I know now that it is why I think the way I do, behave the way I do, why I am the person that I am—different from all others as we all must finally be. And I know now that is why more and more as I get older, my function must be that of the rememberer, the celebrator of the pieties of time and place—the past that I came out of yet was not a part of, the town, the county which owned me and will own me all the days of my life. It is finally the reason that I write what I do and as I do—of the old times, the old tales, of both sorrow and joy, with the present knowledge and blessing they continually confer. It is finally the reason—I know it now—that I tell all my tales or—if you will—sing all my songs, and especially this one now.

3
MODERN TIMES

I HAVE SUGGESTED that the breakup of the Drake family began with the death of my grandmother in 1917, but perhaps that may be too sweeping an assertion. Certainly, the family survived and flourished on into the 1920s and 1930s, and my grandfather did not die until 1938. Thus the tale was by no means over and done with when I arrived on the scene in 1930. Rather, it seemed to me as I grew up that the surviving members of the family were inclined to dwell more and more on the past in their thoughts and in their conversation, certainly in their tales. And more and more they seemed to explore (retreat?) into that golden, Arcadian world which might never have existed except in their own minds. I know this was the way I felt when I was young; the past could never have been that golden, that serene, that pure. Surely, they were manufacturing a myth.

Of course there was some truth in their valedictory attitude. The world they had known was very much on the defensive, if not in retreat. Farming had changed; the country had changed; the times had changed; they themselves had changed. And nothing would ever bring them back to their former state. At times I found their attitude toward the past—and especially toward their loved ones already long gone—downright exasperating: romantic, unrealistic, a mirage, one might call it. What had it all to do, anyhow, with me, who was trying to live in the here and now? What did I want with all those ghosts, those dreams?

I had to get a lot older to know, had to see the family almost all die off (at least my father's generation) before I would understand, and then I began to comprehend, but more by fits and starts than directly and straightforwardly. Gradually, I began to see that their seeming retreats into a past I could never enter were not just attempts at a quixotic escapism but, rather, journeys that they found perpetually refreshing and renewing because these forays brought them into touch with what had been the real source of strength, the real inspiration of their lives: the home place and all that went with it. I wished I had had something of that experience—something which would be to me what the home place had been and still was to the Drakes—but I was inevitably shut out from that world, to some extent: I lived in a different world from theirs—a modern world with lots of conveniences, certainly, but one which, even then in the rural South, was becoming progressively more depersonalized and regimented, though not overnight, not dramatically, to be sure. But already the cloud was in the sky, no bigger than a man's hand.

On the other hand, it was surely the disparity between the Drakes' times and my own that began to work on my sensibility and made me early begin to ask the questions and pose the riddles I have tried to come to terms with here and in many of my other literary endeavors. I grew up and left home; I went off to school, first to Vanderbilt and then to Yale. Then I spent some years teaching in the Midwest (an alien land indeed) before I went to teach in Texas (less alien of course but different, too) and finally returned to Tennessee. By then I had seen enough of other cultures to appreciate just what it was the Drakes had, just what it was they had given me. But I had to travel—step outside the picture frame of my life—before I could know this. I think it was no accident that I began writing my first stories when I was living in Michigan.

I became aware of the Drake world then and knew more about what my inheritance was than ever before, but, by the same token, I could see it vanishing or else being transmuted into something else,

Robert Drake's uncles and father (right) left him a "legacy of life and joy and love."

and not always into something rich and strange either. I saw my uncles and my father die, but also I saw the social and economic changes that were taking place in our county and in our town; they were changes that, in many ways, would make impossible any future heritage like that of the Drakes. I saw families and communities falling apart; they were highly mobile, highly "efficient," to be sure, but often lacking in fundamental cohesiveness or coherence. I saw the church, the home no longer necessarily central to life in that world, and I saw the impious efforts of man at work to deface or obliterate not only his own past but also the natural world around him. I saw people treated more and more as statistics and the fruits of the earth more and more as commodities. I saw the end of the Drake world.

O, we are not altogether played out as a family. I have cousins who have produced issue, and the name will go on, but we now are scattered almost literally to the four winds. Few of us, I think, can say that there is the real center to our lives that our fathers seem to have found in the home place. The pieces which follow now are, therefore, almost necessarily elegiac, yet I do not want to be thought of as completely ringing down the curtain on the Drake drama here. We are still alive and kicking, most of us; and we all remember with affection our fathers and their love for their family, their reverence for their heritage. We know that we will carry such memories with us all our lives and cherish them tenderly. But we know, too, that our lives are, in some respects, diminished in comparison with theirs; we feel that we have somehow missed out on a lot which they held almost by right, and that makes us sad. But we remain forever grateful for these memories and the great gift we feel we have been given by our fathers—their legacy of life and joy and love.

❧ Portrait in Black and White

THERE WAS NEVER ANYTHING Laodicean about the Drakes: their word was always yea, yea and nay, nay. Of course, this was all back before my time; but I have heard how stubborn and *contrary* (accented of course on the second syllable) Pa Drake could be when he took a notion. I do not know whether it had anything to do with his being a Confederate veteran; but, after all, when you have fought at Spottsylvania Courthouse and been at Appomattox and all the rest—to say nothing of emigrating to West Tennessee afterwards when it was still pretty much the tall and uncut—you are bound more or less to be affected.

Of course Pa had been a dyed-in-the-wool Virginia Baptist, as I have said. Whenever we went to any kind of event at the Baptist church at Woodville, Mr. Sam Chism, who was the Sunday school superintendent there and sort of the unofficial meeter and greeter for the congregation (Mamma said he was there every time there was a crack in the church door), would have something to say about how sad it was that all those good Drakes (after all, Pa and Grandma had had seven children), had been lost to the Baptist Church. That did not seem to bother Daddy, and it certainly did not disturb Mamma who, on more than one occasion, announced that she was certainly not a *denominationalist*. When I was little, I thought that a fascinating and somehow terrifying word, like *orthodox* and, later on, *eschatalogical*. They certainly had more to do with their time than worry about the one true church or anything else like that. As far as he was concerned, Daddy said, as long as you accepted Jesus Christ as your personal savior, you were home free and, if they would just put the mourner's benches back in the churches (instead of telling people every Sunday how good they all were), then things would start to straighten out. As for anybody that believed that people were naturally good and only led astray by the corrupt world or whatever, well, the more fool they and the less said about that the better.

The Drakes all had strong convictions, and even Grandma was not without considerable steel in her backbone. I know they always loved telling the tale about the time Pa had come to town to get groceries for her but could not find the kind of flour she liked (I think it was Omega) and carried home a sack of some other sort. Grandma made him take it right back to town because she said she was not using an off-brand or one that she had had no experience with. She was a great baker, too, and always made five different kinds of cake at Christmas.

It was Pa who was the real caution when he got his mind made up. Mainly I remember him as an old man of whom I was afraid: age itself can be terrifying to youth, especially when wearing a mustache, as Pa did. When he got older, one of the things he took an especial dislike to was taking a bath. I do not know whether it was all a holdover from his childhood in Virginia and, later on, his living at Maple Grove on the farm where the best you could do was to bathe in a big washtub in front of the fire before it went out at night, or sometimes just take spit-baths out of a bowl. But Pa seemed almost constitutionally opposed to soap and water as such. Not that he wanted to be dirty or smelly, I believe, but somehow he must have thought bathing was beneath his dignity or something like that. I know they always had a difficult time getting him cleaned up to go to the Confederate reunions every year and then, when he came home, getting him to wash off all the grime because he apparently had not bathed while he was gone. Part of this may have been due to the fact that Grandma was gone and none of the sons who survived could be so forceful with him as she had been. They did the best they could, especially about sending him to the reunions, along with Uncle Jack Winbush who was to keep an eye on him and anybody else that came along too.

I have in my possession today a photograph of Pa and another old Confederate veteran from our county when they were all dressed up

Old Mr. Buchanan, Pa Drake,
and Uncle Jack.

down at the railroad station waiting to go off to the reunion; Uncle Jack is standing right beside them, wearing his Confederate badges too. Of course, Uncle Jack, as a Negro, had gone off to the war as his master's body servant, but he was as stout an old soldier as any of the rest of them. One time when Pa and old Mr. Buchanan, I think it was, went to the reunion, which was in Memphis that year, Uncle Jack went along, too, to look after them. But when they went to check in at the dormitory where they were to stay, somebody raised an objection to Uncle Jack's staying in the same room with Pa and the others, whereupon Pa told them that if Uncle Jack could not stay, neither he nor Mr. Buchanan would either. And that was the end of that. (Daddy would get tickled every time he looked at that photograph of the three old Confederates; he said he bet that they did not have fifty dollars among them but that that would not have held them back, anymore than it did the Confederacy itself.)

My friends outside the South often do not know what to make of this story about Pa and Mr. Buchanan and Uncle Jack. They express disbelief, indeed almost consternation, when I tell them that when

Uncle Jack died he had the biggest Negro funeral ever put on in Woodville, complete with a procession downtown around the square. And his coffin was covered with the Confederate flag! Of course they know nothing of the intimacy that existed between the two races in the old days, and it is very difficult to explain it to them now: they cannot imagine how you could have held affection and esteem for somebody who was not allowed to vote or even use the same public facilities. Or else they will counter with the observation that the old relationship might have been a warm and personal one but that it was all based on white condescension and patronage and therefore ultimately demeaning and debasing to both sides.

I will not enter into that question here, but I will say that I saw my first movies while seated in my beloved nurse Louella's lap in the colored gallery of our local picture show (the Dixie Theater). She even taught me to imitate Mae West's saying "Come up and see me some time." Later on, she would go to Memphis with us when we went to shop, and she always went up with us to the dining room on Gerber's fifth floor (the store where Mamma always liked to shop because, she said, it was so genteel). Louella was not allowed to eat in the dining room but was instead directed to the kitchen, and of course I always ate with her there because it was certainly more interesting than eating out front with all those old white folks.

When such stories are told to outsiders, I think they are nearly always misconstrued and quite often downright disbelieved for not fitting any preexisting stereotypes. But this has all gotten off the track of how stubborn and hardheaded (which may well be the other side of the coin from loyalty and devotion, of course) the Drakes could be when they took a notion. A few years ago, when I was home on a visit, someone—I cannot remember who—observed to me, "You know, your Daddy loved three things in the world: the Methodist Church, the Democratic party, and the St. Louis Cardinals." There was some justification for that as far as his institutional loyalties went. Daddy loved the Methodist Church dearly, and he was saddened when the northern and southern branches of the church were amalgamated in 1939. Not only did the southern church (the Methodist Episcopal Church, South, as it was then called) lose a lot of its traditional terminology (with "presiding elder"

becoming "district superintendent" and "Sunday school" turned
into "church school") but Daddy also thought there was a falling off
in orthodoxy, too, under the new dispensation. Certainly, they had
lost all the glorious old line of preachers who had flourished in the
southern church—men like Bishop U. V. W. (the U stood for Urban)
Darlington who once came to hold a revival at Maple Grove up in
the hot summertime wearing a black alpaca suit and long winter
underwear, that could be seen when he was sitting down stuffed into
his high-top shoes. Daddy said that anybody who took so little note
of how he looked and how he felt was bound to be a good preacher,
and he was, I think.

The Democratic party was second only to the church in Daddy's
affections. All his life he would speak of Republicans as though they
were a sort of vermin: "You know there're just *lots* of Republicans up
in East Tennessee." I well remember the first time I ever saw one;
there were only two families in our whole county who would profess
in public to being Republicans. I was almost surprised to learn that
they did not have horns, hoofs, and tails but, instead, looked pretty
much like anybody else. You could have called the Republicans the
party of the conservatives (which Daddy naturally was) until you
were blue in the face, but, as far as Daddy was concerned, the
Republican party was the party of big business, high prices, and
nothing for the farmer. He had heard William Jennings Bryan speak
once and had never gotten over that either, and he could quote from
the "Cross of Gold" speech at the drop of a hat. Bryan was vindicated
all right, Daddy said, when he came to Tennessee to argue against
that *infidel* (another terrible word), Clarence Darrow, at the Scopes
trial, and he died in his sleep while he was there, convinced of his
righteous stand, no matter what the smart-aleck, godless reporters
from up north said.

Daddy could never be other than loyal to the Democratic party,
but in 1928, it was particularly difficult because Al Smith was
running for president and Daddy could not vote for a Roman Catho-
lic. ("Who does the Pope think he is, anyway, always making
speeches 'to the world'?") But he could not betray the party, he said,
and vote for Hoover. Therefore neither he nor Mamma voted at all.
This was different from 1948 when the Dixiecrats tried to secede,

did secede really, and put up candidates of their own on the States' Rights platform. Daddy thought that was all a lot of foolishness; anybody with the sense God gave a billy goat, he said, could see that Harry Truman was a good man who knew his own mind and was not beholden to anybody. Uncle Buford has told me that Daddy was about the only other person in the country besides Truman himself that said he was going to win; Daddy said it all along, according to Uncle Buford.

The St. Louis Cardinals were almost as important, too; they were *his* big-league ball team, the closest one to him down in West Tennessee, and he never missed one of their broadcasts. Strangely enough, he did not seem eager to see the Cardinals as much as to hear them. Occasionally, he would go to St. Louis to market and sometimes take in a ball game, but he did not make it his first priority. It was almost as though if he saw the game it would spoil it for him; listening was better because then he could imagine all he wanted to. But for every game broadcast in the summer he would draw up one of our high-back rockers beside his radio out on the front porch, pull up a coal scuttle to spit in, then light one of his big cigars alternately to chomp, chew, and smoke (all depending on how the game was going), and then he was in business and ready for the game. Naturally, he talked back and forth with whoever was passing by; they would ask and he would tell them how the game was going. (He would not have given a nickel for a house without a front porch where he could sit and see folks go by.) From time to time, he would talk back to the sportscaster on the radio too; he would give advice about what the "Cards" or the "Redbirds" should have done, argue, interpret, cajole, cheer, indeed do almost everything but cry. He wanted *his* team to do well, and he assumed an almost proprietary interest in the players.

What all this adds up to, I suppose, is that all the Drakes were great loyalists—to God, to their duty, to what they believed to be right. And they were none of them ever afraid to stand up and be counted. Far be it from them ever to come whining after the event and say it ought to have been done some other way; they did their talking while the talking was good, and they never backed down. Occasionally, that got them into trouble, even alienated some of their friends, but it never disturbed them. Daddy would say, "I can sleep at night; I can look in the mirror; I can walk down the street and look my fellow man in the eye because I know that I have been honest and straightforward in all my dealings." This was no vain boast; it was simply a statement of fact. Sure, they knew their limitations. They were not especially well-to-do; they were not highly educated; they were not enormously successful in the world. (Uncle Buford would always say about the store, Drake Brothers, "Well, it's just what we've made. We might have done better, but we made it all ourselves. And there it is.") But they had their good name, the most valuable possession of all. There they were: just themselves and not quite like anybody else. And you could take them or leave them, but, no matter what, you always knew where the Drakes stood; and above all, you always knew they were there.

❧ *Pure Gold*

MY UNCLE WESLEY, who lived down at Barfield, six miles below Woodville, was Daddy's second oldest brother—right after Uncle John. He was really the best looking of all the Drakes, for he was tall and slim and erect, with patrician features and iron gray hair. I thought he always seemed kind, if a little abstracted, in his day-to-day encounters, as if his mind was really on something else and he was not altogether living within the here and now. He was dignity and decorum personified, serious in a way the other Drakes never were, almost as though he was afraid to laugh. And that was not like them at all.

He behaved as he did because he had had so much trouble, Mamma said, and she respected him because of what he had come through and lived to tell (Mamma's judgments about people often were based on that criterion). For one thing, Uncle Wesley had left Maple Grove as soon as he finished high school and had gone to work in Barfield, which was only a wide place in the middle of the road, rather than to Woodville. That was two strikes against him right off, Mamma said, because not much of anybody was down there except a bunch of widows and old maids, many of them quite well-to-do, all living by themselves in great big houses, with nothing better to do than keep tabs on one another's every movement and speculate on the whys and wherefores every time one of the others stuck his head out the door. Even Daddy, as loyal as he was, said it was the sort of place you could easily spend a week in during a single afternoon; nothing there ever seemed to change, and the most excitement any of those old women ever had, or even thought of, was getting all dressed up in the afternoon and going to the drugstore for a Coca-

Cola. Every time we passed through there on the way to Memphis, Mamma would say, well, that was something else she had to be thankful for: we did not live in Barfield.

Of course, years later I came to see that there might be a virtue in Barfield's quietness and imperviousness to change. Whereas I hardly knew anybody mentioned in the Woodville locals of the weekly *Gazette* anymore, I could always turn to the Barfield column, no matter how far off I then lived or how many years later it was, and the same people were still doing the same things on the same days of the week as they had been doing twenty-five years before—spending the day shopping in Memphis or visiting (or being visited by) their relatives in Blytheville, Arkansas, or Corinth, Mississippi. It was really a lot like Cranford or one of Jane Austen's quiet villages, and it gave a measure of order and serenity to the turbulent years that were accumulating around me. Woodville and the big wide world might change, but I always knew I could count on Barfield. Indeed, just a few months ago the old hotel there (the one that the three Pleasants sisters, all old maids of course, ran for years) burned up and the one fire engine the town possessed got too close to the fire because the driver and other firemen (all volunteers of course) were too busy talking to the crowd to notice, and it burned up too! As I said, Barfield never changes.

Uncle Wesley elected to go to work in the Barfield Bank and Trust Company. Of course he taught a class in the Methodist Sunday School, was assiduous in his duties in the bank, and soon came to be regarded as an exemplary young man who was no doubt going places (though by this they never meant that he would leave Barfield: why would anyone want to do that?). There was general approval when he became engaged to Marion Lloyd, whose mother kept the boarding house where Uncle Wesley roomed. Of course the Lloyds were Baptists and that might have been a handicap, but Pa Drake had originally been a Baptist, so that was not all so foreign to the Drakes as it might have been. Aunt Marion did not try to convert Uncle Wesley; she left him alone as long as he left her free to go to her own church because, as she used to say, she was a Baptist "from the crown of her head to the soles of her feet," which could have been a reference to the Baptist doctrine of total immersion but was, more probably, just her way of being emphatic. Therefore one of Uncle Wesley's troubles was not having a wife in his own church even after he got to be Sunday school superintendent; Mamma always said that put him almost in a false position but there was nothing he could do about it.

But that was not his biggest trouble by any means. Some years after they were married, Aunt Marion died of pneumonia, leaving Uncle Wesley with two small children, my cousins Anne and Tom, to bring up. There was nothing else for him to do but move back to Mrs. Lloyd's (she had quit taking in boarders by then) and see her bring up his children in the Baptist church and preside over his life in every possible way. I suppose he never had a chance to say "boo" about any of it. Not that he was overawed by Mrs. Lloyd or anything like that (he respected her enormously), but he was too bereaved just then and too dignified always to do anything else. He was a widower with two small children, and life was too serious for him even to smile or laugh, much less assert himself forcefully. He made the living, Mrs. Lloyd reared the children, and that was their life.

The situation was bound to take the starch out of him, Mamma said, and that seemed to be true because to me Uncle Wesley always seemed strait-laced, almost prim—not forbidding but very much on his dignity and seemingly impervious to fun—and that was not like the Drakes at all. O, occasionally, he would launch out with a sally or two, but then almost immediately his dignity would reassert itself as though he could not afford otherwise. One time the Drake brothers all drove to Uncle Seaton Burks' funeral in Wilmington (twenty miles north of Woodville), and as they were leaving afterwards, Uncle Wesley, without thinking, said to Uncle Seaton's surviving children, "Well, be good," which was the Drakes' perennial formula of light-hearted farewell. Then of course all the brothers got tickled and began to giggle at the inappropriateness of his remark, and Uncle Wesley, who by that time was scandalized by his own words as well as his brothers' behavior, said to Uncle Jim, who was driving, "Just drive on out of town as fast as you can. I'll pay the fine."

Another time Uncle Wesley went to a bankers' convention in Chicago, and one of the extra added attractions featured was a trip up to Milwaukee by boat on Lake Michigan. Uncle Wesley, who in the most aggrieved yet dignified tones would protest that he had been dreadfully seasick ("I was sick, just deathly sick"), could nevertheless be extremely amusing about his own home remedies for such indispositions: lie perfectly flat on your back in your berth with a wet towel on your forehead and pray that you would just live to get back on dry land one more time and promise never to leave it again if the Good Lord spared you. Uncle Wesley took his pleasures sadly anyway. Why, he said, on Sundays, with no work to do, he often got so restless and bored that he would develop the headache and have to take two aspirins.

The role that seemed to fit him best was that of the dignified, scandalized widower who found it difficult to manage domestic difficulties. And as such he was not so much funny in himself (he was too discomfited for that) as the source of fun for others. For instance, there was the time when he came to one of the famous Drake Christmas dinners at our house, bringing of course Anne and Tom with him, and Tom refused to eat the turkey and dressing or anything else. Uncle Wesley was mortified, but Daddy as usual was all heart and asked what Tom liked to eat at home. Uncle Wesley said Tom was always a finicky eater but, if anything, he liked cold biscuits and molasses. With that Daddy went out to the kitchen and brought back the molasses jug and some cold biscuits left over from the night before and set them down in front of Tom, who proceeded to wade right into them there and then. And Uncle Wesley was scandalized. Mamma, I might add, was right peeved; she was enormously proud of her cooking, and rightly so.

Another time the whole family (including me, at six months old listed as "infant son" in the newspaper account) had gathered at the Harmony Methodist Church, which Uncle John was serving then, for Mary Virginia's wedding (she was his and Aunt Estelle's only daughter). There was a feisty little boy who lived next door to the parsonage who wanted my cousin, Stuart, Uncle John's younger son, to come out and fight him. But Stuart declined on the grounds that, because he was so much older than the little boy, it would not be a fair contest. However, he volunteered the information that he had a little cousin (Tom, who, along with Anne, had come from Barfield with Uncle Wesley for the wedding) in the house who would be only too glad to take him on. So he called Tom to come out, and sure enough Tom, who was always ready for a fight, was delighted to oblige; he almost pulverized his opponent, and again Uncle Wesley was scandalized.

I do not believe that Anne ever gave Uncle Wesley any pause as being an affront to his dignity as a bereaved widower. She was too quiet and self-controlled for that (Tom was quiet but apparently not always self-controlled). But Uncle Wesley did worry about what she would think of him, I believe. Did he regard her as a kind of stand-in for her dead mother or for her grandmother, Mrs. Lloyd, who was very much alive? Did he feel that she was there to monitor his behavior, to see that he lived up to expectations or something like that? He always seemed to tread warily around her, as though he was afraid of not coming up to the mark where she was concerned. He obviously loved her deeply, but his tenderness for her always seemed somehow touched with gravity, even apprehension: he had lost her mother but he would *not* lose her.

This was particularly true after Uncle Wesley began courting Miss Emily Herron, who was a well-to-do old maid who lived all alone at her family's big old place (she always called it "out home") in the country. She had been a good friend of Aunt Marion's and she was another good Baptist. So there was no reason why any of Aunt Marion's family or anybody else would object to their courtship, but what would Anne think of it all, Uncle Wesley must have wondered. She was old enough to remember her mother and perhaps might think him disloyal to her memory if he remarried. Even though she knew Miss Emily well and knew that she had been a good friend of her mother's, she might resent her. Uncle Wesley therefore never told her a thing about his intentions but left that all to Mrs. Lloyd, her grandmother. However, he did caution Uncle John, who was to perform the ceremony, and Uncle Jim, who was to "stand up" with him, not to drive to Miss Emily's through Barfield but to go by the back road. Who knew what folks in Barfield (Anne especially) might not think if they were to see them driving together through town?

Uncle John and Uncle Jim did as he had told them, and nobody in Barfield knew anything for certain right then, though of course it had been an open secret for quite some time that Uncle Wesley was going to marry Miss Emily. Anne did miss her father that night and wondered where he was, but the next morning Mrs. Lloyd told her he had gotten married and had gone to Memphis on his honeymoon. Anne had apparently already put two and two together and seemed not to be surprised at all; she did not turn a hair.

Typically it was Uncle Wesley who was the most scandalized of all in connection with the marriage. When he was telling Uncle Jim of his intentions beforehand, he asserted, "Miss Emily is one of the finest women in the world. She's just as fine as gold; she's just pure gold." Uncle Jim, without batting an eye, replied, "Well, you better watch out then, Little Bubber. Roosevelt's liable to call her in!" This was back in the thirties of course, and Uncle Wesley, thoroughly understanding the allusion, was appropriately scandalized. Aunt Emily was indeed a fine woman, if somewhat still the perennial old maid, and they seemed happily married until his death twenty years later. Of course, she never called him anything but "Mr. Drake," and he always referred to her as "Miss Emily," but they were really devoted to each other, I believe. When he was no longer a widower with two small children, all living with his Baptist mother-in-law, he grew less scandalized by life, I think, and more and more just sat back and enjoyed it as much as any of the other Drakes. And that of course is saying a very great deal.

❧ King Lear at Maple Grove

I REMEMBER PA DRAKE only as a very old man of course. (He lived past ninety-two.) And I was always a little afraid of him, mainly because of his age and his big walrus mustache, which somehow seemed foreign and sinister in my world. Surely no one could have gone through the final campaign with the Army of Northern Virginia as he had, been present and "paroled" at Appomattox Courthouse, and then emigrated to West Tennessee in the late 1860s without being a formidable character. But then to have lived so long afterwards! Was not that something of an anticlimax for him?

I know that Pa had been born to higher things than he was later to live among. His family had been well-to-do slave-owners, and he had run away from school—an "academy"—to join the Confederate Army, as his older brother (Uncle Werter, who was later to become a doctor and serve as the school physician to Hollins College) had already done. Uncle Werter is buried in Ballsville, Virginia, in the Mt. Moriah Cemetery (and I have seen his grave). Uncle John inherited the gold-headed cane that Hollins presented him with when he retired, and that was the thing that made him seem absolutely real to me; a grave, after all, is very impersonal.

Anyhow, Pa was very much to the manner born, and I have often thought it took considerable courage for him to pull up stakes as he did and come out to West Tennessee, which was still like the frontier then; it was rough, ragged territory where General Forrest and his troops had fought the Yankees through many a skirmish and where the Fort Pillow "massacre" had taken place, all not too far from the Shiloh battlefield. I do not know why Pa picked West Tennessee to

126

settle in; it certainly could not have been described to him by any returned traveler as an Eldorado. Perhaps it was as far as his imagination could take him from Virginia (just this side of the Mississippi River, remember) without committing him to the utter finality of Texas or California. Anyhow, he and one of his first cousins (on the Ball side of the family) came out from Virginia, getting off the train at Johnson's Station, twenty miles to the east, because in those days the railroad had not come to Woodville. I do not know what their idea was—farming, cutting timber, or whatever—but the cousin soon got a job teaching school, stayed for only a year (to earn his fare back to Virginia), and then went home to get married and settle down. And Pa did not see him again for forty years, when he went back to Richmond for the Confederate reunion.

Somewhere along the line, though, Pa, who was William Ball Drake, met my grandmother, who was born Elizabeth Ann Burks, began to court her, and eventually married her. Although, as I have said, I do not have anything definite to go on here, I always imagined that he came from socially better folks than she did. His people were decidedly Virginia aristocrats, even if they did belong to the Baptist rather than the Episcopal Church. His photographs show him as grand in feature and demeanor, with the firm bones and aquiline profile of the thoroughbred, every inch a gentleman. Grandma's family were from the rung below them in the social ladder, I think—small landholders who might never have owned slaves but fiercely independent and beholden to no man. Ironically, it was "Betty" and her family who put food on the table while Pa sat out on the front porch and talked about old times in the Old Dominion.

They lived first on a little farm Grandma had inherited near Barfield; then later, around the turn of the century, they sold it to buy the farm at Maple Grove that all the Drakes later referred to as the home place. ("Home" as such was wherever they were living at the time, and when they spoke of that, it could mean either place. The "home place," on the other hand, always meant Maple Grove because that was where most of them grew to adulthood, and it was from there that they went out into the world on their own to try their wings. It was there that they all longed for when they were homesick, even many years later.) Pa apparently made a stab at doing subsistence farming, but it was Grandma who really managed and made ends meet. This is evident in the many photographs of the family that exist. Grandma seems demure, shy, hardly ever looking directly at the camera, but by no means weak; it is as though she is too careful and troubled about many things and has no time for such frivolities right then. On the other hand, Pa looks at the camera head-on, boldly, as though to suggest that, no matter what state he may have fallen into, he is still William Ball Drake from Ballsville, Virginia. But always he is untidy, with his collar often open and his boots unpolished. (Did he think, after all those years, that he was still slumming?) I think everybody in the Maple Grove community thought highly of my grandparents, though: if "Bill" was still the Virginia gentleman, everybody knew that it was "Betty" who was the wheel behind the wheel, despite the fact that she was a born homebody with little taste for social, not to say public, life.

Pa's kinfolks came to visit from time to time, and once even his mother came; she had packed her trunk by the simple expedient of rolling up all her clothes and throwing them in in no particular order. (This was the same trunk that she took hams that she had cured at home down to Richmond in every fall, selling them so that she could buy some new clothes for the season. The Balls and the Drakes might have been reduced in circumstances since the war, but they were still keeping up appearances and paying their own way.) Pa's sister, Aunt Laura Hurt, also came. She was the biggest Baptist of them all and, along with all her children, a champion visitor. One of the Richmond cousins said that when he came home at night he never knew which Hurt was going to be in the bed with him.

I do not know what the Virginia folks thought of Grandma. Of course they had to make some allowance for her being a Methodist, but I do not believe they ever condescended to her; she might have been quiet, but she was not the kind to take anything off anybody. They must have had sense enough to see that it was she who really kept things going at home.

Pa was a born talker and fraternizer. When he was not coming into Woodville to get the latest news of the world, local or otherwise, he was writing letters to newspaper editors about all manner of topics—

Aunt Laura Hurt (right) was a "champion visitor" to the home place. Pictured here with her are (left to right) the author's father, Uncle Buford, Eashel, and Pa Drake.

political, social, religious, whatever. (Once, toward the end of his life, he even wrote a "tribute" to a prominent citizen of Woodville who had taken his own life, urging the public to forgive and forget the manner of his death—suicide still carried a moral stigma then—and to remember only the integrity of his life and the beauty of his character.) And there was always the war—there was only one—for him to talk about.

I realize that I may be making Pa sound like a crashing bore here, which he most certainly was not. He simply liked to talk rather than to work, and he was always ready to attend to anybody's business but his own, something like Rip Van Winkle. Of course it was from him that my father and his brothers all got their love of tale-telling, their love of jokes, their love of fun. Characteristically, his recurring nightmare (which he never tired of relating to all) was suddenly to find himself in church stark naked. (Grandma was simply too busy for such carrying on, though I gather that she was not without humor of the quiet, domestic sort and indeed was not incapable of deflating Pa when he soared too high in some of his flights: she told him once that if the Confederacy had fought as hard as they *talked* about fighting, things might have gone quite differently.)

She died at the age of sixty-two, an age which in 1917, particularly on the farm, everybody thought made her an old woman. My father said she had simply worked herself to death, but Uncle Buford said it was grief for her younger daughter who had died the preceding summer that gave her the fatal blow. However you looked at it, though, you could not help seeing Grandma as some sort of Martha, too busy to sit and talk yet loving and suffering those who did. The brothers all adored her, too, and could never in years to come speak of her without tears. They respected Pa of course; that went without saying. But did they sometimes resent, without ever being aware of it, his easy-goingness, even what might have been called his laziness, his letting Grandma do most of the work? After all, you could not make a life's work out of being William Ball Drake from Ballsville, Virginia, and a Confederate veteran.

But then Pa, who of course had never been other than a faithful husband if a scanty provider, did the strangest and (to the Drakes) the most outrageous thing of all. Within a year of Grandma's death, he married her sister, Aunt Fannie, who was a widow with children more or less the same ages as the Drakes. The Drakes were simply scandalized, but I do not know how Aunt Fannie's children took it. Of course, it was more a marriage of convenience than anything else (Pa was simply lonesome), but his sons could never regard it as anything but an act of disloyalty to their mother and her memory despite their quite genuine affection for their aunt. Indeed, so embarrassed and hurt by it all was my father that he never spoke directly to me about it in his life. I only learned of the marriage from one of my older cousins when I was nearly grown. I did hear Daddy once call some old man who had remarried before the funeral baked meats for his first wife were hardly cold "an old fool to embarrass his children that way. . . . I know myself what it's like to have a father do that." Then he immediately hushed and would say no more. Even then—I was still in my teens—I realized that he was torn between two different emotions: love for his father and hurt and bewilderment at his conduct. And I think I came closer in that moment to understanding him than I ever had before, not as my father but as a man.

Pa's marriage to Aunt Fannie, during which they lived at her place on the other side of Maple Grove and Pa rented out the home place, did not last long. They never got a divorce; he merely went back to the home place to live, first by himself, then with a "good, plain" family that farmed the place for him and agreed to keep an eye on the old man as part of their bargain. I never knew exactly how and why Pa and Aunt Fannie broke up until recently, when one of the cousins (Aunt Fannie's granddaughter) told me how it happened. Pa was getting ready to go off to the annual Confederate reunion, which was going to be held that year in Birmingham, and he was unable to find his new shirt that he wanted to take with him. When he asked Aunt Fannie where it was, she told him she had just washed and ironed it and put it in his bureau drawer. But he said it was not there and, as was characteristic with him, the more firmly Aunt Fannie said she had put the shirt there, the more vehemently he denied that she had ever done so. Finally, Aunt Fannie had had enough, and she said, "Well, you obviously don't believe me. Would you have believed Betty?" When Pa snapped out, "Yes, indeed," Aunt Fannie replied, "Well, if that's the way you feel, you can just take your things out of here and *git!*" Pa stomped out of the house and took the train for the reunion and never came back there.

Daddy and Uncle Buford had not wanted him to go to the reunion; he always ate too much (he never drank), kept late hours, and came home half dead. But this time his indignation at Aunt Fannie (and perhaps at himself, too) was too much for him, and he threw caution to the winds. On the way back home, he staggered into Uncle John's, who was preaching on a circuit near Memphis then, and announced he felt so bad that he was probably going to die but, whatever they did, not to tell Daddy and Uncle Buford (who of course did not then know about his separation from Aunt Fannie). Uncle John and Aunt Estelle had what Mamma called a parrot-monkey time with Pa, trying to get him first into the bathtub and then into bed; if there was anything Pa hated worse than going to bed in the daytime, it was taking a bath (just like a little boy). Finally they succeeded, and the doctor came and diagnosed him as worn out more than anything else; Pa then told them about him and Aunt Fannie, and as a result Daddy and Uncle Buford finally learned all about it anyway.

That was when Pa went back to the home place to live, with the tenant family to look after him, and that was when I first remember him as very old and deaf and always smelling of the tobacco smoke from his pipe. And, as I said before, I was afraid of him, as much for his great age as anything, as though he were some primordial creature left over from prehistoric times but even then also something of a *memento mori*. A few years later, though, Pa fell and broke his hip. Then he became a semi-invalid (the break never healed properly). So there seemed nothing else to do but move him up the road to Uncle Jim and Aunt Mary's, where Daddy and Uncle Buford built a room onto the house for him. Pa loved Aunt Mary dearly as she was the daughter of the cousin who had first come to West Tennessee with him, and he called her "Marianna" as a pet name most of the time. She was devoted to him, indulging him in his fancies, as when he told them he was sure they could trade in their old Model A on a new Ford with very little balance to pay because it still ran so well. Aunt Mary told him she would not trade that old car in for anything; it was so old that it was almost valuable as an antique. She and Uncle Jim would sit patiently and listen to him talk (he never rambled) by the hour about the war. One of his favorite stories was about the last Christmas of the war (in 1864) when the Union and the Confederate lines were camped so close to each other around Richmond that they sang Christmas carols back and forth.

He was almost stone deaf then (he could hear pretty well if you sat beside him and talked to him alone, but hearing in a crowd was impossible for him), and he could not walk without assistance; the doctor told them to keep him out of the bed, however, because old people went quickly when they took to their beds, he said. They and all the rest of the family did their best to divert him, going out every Sunday afternoon to see him and never for a moment acting as though it was a duty. (And really, I do not believe they considered it as such.) And they kept him out of the bed, too, helping him from his bed to the old high-back rocker that he always sat in. He never wanted for anything; all the brothers saw to that. His every material need they satisfied, and they did what they could for the inner man as well. The Methodist preacher on that circuit came to see him from time to time, and once they even got Mr. Oscar Hickman, who carried the mail on that route and was a fine guitar player, to come play and sing for him. Even now I can hear his "Strawberry Roan"

Right: *Pa Drake, around 1935, as his grandson Robert first remembers him.*

Below: *Uncle Jim and Aunt Mary's home. Pa Drake's room is pictured at right.*

echoing in the quiet summer night on the dark front porch (that was before TVA and the closest lamp was in the living room). Sometimes Pa would sing all by himself old songs like "Lorena" and "Tenting on the Old Camp Ground." And always of course they would listen patiently when he talked about the war.

I did not think Pa would ever die: he was too old, had lived through too much, and should therefore have been immune to mortality, it seemed. But he finally did die, when I was seven years old. The day he died, they all knew he was sinking fast. He had pneumonia at the end—what they used to call "the old man's

Pa Drake in his final days.

friend," and the doctor said his lungs were "filling up" quickly. So Mamma and Aunt Janie, Uncle Buford's wife, went out to Uncle Jim and Aunt Mary's. Of course there was nothing they could do except be there; but that was important enough. (It would have been difficult for Daddy and Uncle Buford to leave the store.) Finally, they drove back into town to tell us Pa was dead, and I could hardly believe it; he had been too permanent a fixture in my life, I thought, and the lives of his children. Daddy did not break down and cry before me (I somehow wanted him to, to show his vulnerability, even at the same time fearing that he would thus show an unmanly weakness), but Mamma said he did later after I had gone out in the yard to play. I did not even go to the funeral; Mamma and Daddy thought I was too young, and I went home that day after school with one of my classmates to stay until they got back. I heard all about the funeral from them though and was surprised to learn that Uncle John, who after all was a Methodist preacher, did not conduct the service himself. However, he did make lots of photographs of Uncle Jim's house and of Pa's room on the day of the funeral, and he took more pictures of the flowers on Pa's grave at the cemetery. There are even pictures of Uncle Jim and his daughter, my cousin Laura, out in the front yard on that beautiful April day, as well as a picture of old Aunt Julie Henning, who lived on the place, when she came up to pay her respects. She had been born into slavery and so was about the same age as Pa, and I was always a little afraid of her, too. (Her

Aunt Julie Henning.

great age and her having been a slave seemed to give her proprietary rights over all the Drakes, and she usually talked to them as though they were children—and not very bright children at that.) They said she came into the front room where Pa was lying in his coffin (I remember hearing that it cost $200, which, I suppose, was a fair enough sum in 1938); she looked down at him for a long time, seeing the aquiline nose, the delicate cheek bones, the long thin fingers now in their final repose, and the sandy-colored hair that had never quite turned gray. Then she said, half to herself and perhaps the other half to Pa, "He sure was a good man." And really there seemed to be nothing else to say.

✖ The News from London

WHEN I WAS IN THE SIXTH GRADE, I went through a phase of eating a very unconventional breakfast. Every morning I would get up and fix myself two pieces of heavily buttered toast, slather them with Monarch peanut butter (the crunchy kind) and Welch's Grapelade, then open a Coca-Cola and take them all back to bed with me on a tray. Years later I asked my mother why she ever let me get away with such behavior and such a breakfast, and she replied, "Because I knew you were getting two well-balanced meals a day at dinner and supper." Perhaps that was her wisest strategy of all: simply to say nothing and wait for me to more or less come to my senses, which I eventually did.

Perhaps the strangest thing of all was that, while I was devouring this bizarre repast (with toast crumbs, peanut butter, and jelly of course smeared all over the bed), I would simultaneously read through my collection of railroad time tables, planning all sorts of imaginary journeys involving elaborate connections and fantastically close changes of trains, and listen on my radio to the war news, which was usually Edward R. Murrow and Charles Collingwood reporting from London on all the damage that had been done there in the blitz the night before.

In those days, transatlantic broadcasting was not so technically efficient as it has since become and I always felt as though they were speaking to us from the other end of a tunnel and we could really imagine that we heard the Atlantic waves billowing tempestuously underneath it all. To tell the truth, such feats—along with transatlantic telephoning, which now seems as simple and clear as talking to Memphis or even down the street—have always seemed greater

Robert Drake's boyhood home, built during the 1870s, where his mother also grew up.

and more thrilling accomplishments to me than walking on the moon, which I still find literally incomprehensible and highly questionable as an achievement anyhow: when you get to the moon, what can you *do* there?

Anyhow, we heard what all had happened in London the night before—how many people had been killed, how many lesser casualties had been inflicted, and, most important, how many German planes the RAF had brought down. I could not help glorying in the English spunk. There they were on that little island, all alone with their backs to the wall (we had barely gotten into the war), brazening it out against Hitler with gallantry (O, that happy few, that band of brothers!) and with bull-dog determination, so formidably and appropriately embodied in the person and utterances of Winston Churchill. I wished them well with all my heart: I believed in Queen Elizabeth I, Sir Francis Drake, the Duke of Wellington, and Lord Nelson, and I could not imagine how anybody could ever ultimately defeat a people who had produced leaders like that.

I know that was the way the Drakes felt, too. Uncle John always said there had been no finer political leaders or men of higher character in public life than Disraeli and Gladstone in the nineteenth century and Asquith and Ramsay MacDonald in the twentieth century. I did not know much about them, but I admired Sir Francis Drake a great deal for his singeing the King of Spain's beard and sailing around the world, and I used to wish I was descended from him until I learned that he never had any legitimate issue; then I changed my mind because I did not want any bastards in my background. (Now I would not give a damn; indeed, I would probably find it amusing.) But when Uncle John and Daddy were discussing the progress of the war, they would always say that the main thing about the English was that they loved their country and that nobody was ever going to push them around or take it away from them. How they gloried in Churchill's defiant boast that fighting would take place on the beaches and in the streets! They could understand fighting to defend your home, the people and the things you loved.

Of course, it could have been pointed out to them that the French and the Germans also loved their respective countries and, presumably, did not want to be pushed around either. I am not sure exactly what they would have said to that except that there was a difference because the Germans never were content with what they had themselves and could not leave other folks alone, and because the French were too busy eating and drinking or whatever (they would not have said *copulating* aloud then, but I'm sure they thought it) to look after their country like they ought to. They said that twice we had had to go over and straighten them all out and that in the future we ought to build a wall around the whole place and let them fight it out among themselves. In these discussions of course England was always an exception; Uncle John and Daddy were loyal defenders of our mother country but never denied that we had been right to break away from them in the Revolutionary War because they had been mistreating us and taking advantage of us then ("no taxation without representation!"). But that was all over and done with, and, after all, England was where our language and many of our institutions had originated and we should therefore always be grateful to them. Our ancestors had come from there, too, even if we were not descended from Sir Francis Drake. (Years later a British immigration officer at Southampton looked at my passport and asked, "Ah, Mr. Drake, are you perhaps related to the Drakes down at Taunton?" I replied, "I should like to think so," which I thought both tactful and noncommittal since I really did not know.) Certainly nobody in his right mind would have ever tried to push Pa Drake or any of his sons around or even for a minute try to take their homes away from them.

What the Drakes ultimately admired most about the English was that they loved their homes. That was the way they still felt about Maple Grove and the home place even if they had all been gone from there for so long a time. Every morning we listened to the radio to hear how London had fared the night before, and in the newsreels at the picture show we saw the bomb damage and the Londoners going down into the Underground every night for shelter. Of course always there was *Life* magazine, which every week brought the whole wide world into our house and we could see it, not just hear it on the radio.

After we got into the war, we did not forget about England; it was that our thoughts turned more to the Pacific, where things were going very badly for us at first. (I remember that on the Sunday night after hearing about Pearl Harbor we drove out to Uncle Jim's at Maple Grove to tell them about it. It was before TVA arrived out there, and their old radio that ran off a battery had not been working well, and we wanted to be sure they knew all about it right away. Uncle Jim and Daddy agreed that it was just as well we had joined the war effort; we would have had to sooner or later, they said, and now we could pitch in and get it over with.) But always we kept at least one ear and one eye on the news from London. After all, the Pacific was a big ocean, and we could afford to give up a lot of it to the Japanese, at least for a while, but we could never let England go. Above all, we could never let Churchill down. Along with Franklin D. Roosevelt, he was one of Daddy's great heroes, and of course his mother had been an American. I do not think Daddy ever held the English Royal Family in such esteem; he was too much a republican (with a small "r" of course) for that. But he did concede that they seemed to be working hard at the job of keeping up morale and that that was very important. They had not left the country either but had stayed home and gotten bombed like everybody else, and in every photograph of the queen and the two young princesses they wore those same blue suits since they had been rationed, too.

The tide finally turned and V-E Day came, but not until after Roosevelt had died, to Daddy's great sorrow. He loved to tell about what he had read concerning an incident in Roosevelt's last days at

Warm Springs, Georgia, where he died. The president had asked his secret service men to drive him up to the top of a nearby mountain and then go off as far as they legally could and leave him alone for a half-hour or so. Daddy said that nobody would ever know for sure but that Roosevelt must have sensed that his death was near and wanted to commune with the Almighty about the state of the country and probably his own state as well. Daddy said he was touched by such "spirituality." In many ways, Roosevelt came out better than Churchill because he died at the very moment of the Allied victory in Western Europe and could presumably go right on to glory in his hour of triumph: Churchill, on the other hand, had to stay around for all the mopping up, and then be turned out of office by a country that seemed ungrateful, to say the least, for all he had done for them. Daddy said he never could understand that but he guessed it was just the Old Adam: people just naturally bit the hand that fed them, which, though not a particularly good advertisement for the human race, was true nevertheless.

Daddy lived to see Churchill back in office again, but he was not alive when I made my first trip to England in 1958—a trip which was to inaugurate one of the few completely realized dreams of my life: to see England myself and find both the land and the people all I had ever hoped they would be. (I was already earning my living by teaching their literature.) Uncle Buford was still going strong then, and he said that he wished that somehow I could get to shake hands with Winston Churchill. Well, of course, I never did that, but I did stand in a crowd outside No. 10 Downing Street and watch him arrive for a big dinner in honor of some visiting dignitary. He was so feeble by then that he had to be helped out of the car, but he turned around to face the crowd, who were applauding him enthusiastically, and gave us his trademark sign: the "V for Victory." And I felt right then that that was enough: I had already gotten my money's worth out of both him and England.

❧ The Forty-Two Game

EVERY NIGHT OF THE WORLD my father would go back downtown to play forty-two. It was a game like dominoes, only played with cards which had to be specially printed in Memphis. Our town was one of the few places where I ever heard of its being played at all, but I think I did hear, when I was growing up, that it was used as a gambling game "out in Texas" (things were always "out" in Texas because it was so big, I supposed, like the "interior" of darkest Africa or something). Years later, when I was teaching in Texas, one of my students told me that forty-two was still played in her home town but played with dominoes, I believe.

The forty-two games in Woodville, when I was growing up, were played night in and night out (including Sundays but not Saturdays, for that was the night the stores all stayed open late to accommodate the farmers who were in from the country) in the offices of the Johnson Coal Company that opened out of the West Side Arcade on the square. In the winter, there was a Heatrola roaring away in the room where they played; it was so hot and fierce that it almost matched the emotions and tempers of the players themselves, and it was stifling to me when as a small boy I would come down to wait on Daddy after the picture show had let out. In summer, they moved the table out into the Arcade (wonderful name! what did it suggest— European architecture and vistas or something else equally exotic?) so as to get the benefit of the drafts and breezes that were always fanning through. No matter the time or the season, the games went on, year after year.

The players were mostly business men, with a lawyer or an occasional doctor thrown in. The game was also played by ladies in

141

the town at the Washington Avenue Forty-two Club, where they met every other Monday night with their husbands. But my father's group was exclusively masculine and held by no fixed organization, never a club, only a group. It was somewhere to go in those days before television and interstates had either confined people to their darkened homes or sent them barreling down the highway to the bright lights of Memphis for their amusement and entertainment. Of course there was always the picture show, but these men were somewhat distrustful of such "brought on" diversions and, on the whole, preferred the company of each other to anything that smacked of the imported. Similarly, my father would never let us patronize a chain store of any sort, because it "took all the money out of town," not leaving any of it behind. O, there was an exception to the movie prejudice now and then: my father was devoted to Nelson Eddy and Jeanette MacDonald, and he never missed one of their singing sagas. But in general he held movies (or, as we then said, picture shows) in low esteem, snorting contemptuously whenever I fell under the influence of some new star and wrote him a letter asking for an autographed picture. They were all no better in that business than they should be, he suggested more than once.

But the forty-two game was an institution in Woodville. There were the regulars like my father who went every night, and there were the floaters, or what Daddy called the "boosters," who were always on hand to observe from the sidelines, occasionally sitting in when one of the regulars was unable to be present but mainly looking on, sometimes even egging on with joke and gibe. I have often wondered why my mother did not object to his being out every night, but she never seemed to mind; she knew where he was, and she could always get in touch with him if she needed to. Her favorite evening diversion, it seemed, was visiting with friends on the telephone since she could not drive and did not want to walk long distances to see them. So I suppose they shared a sort of truce between them: he would tolerate the telephone visiting if she would allow the forty-two game. Truly I think they were happy in the arrangement. They saw as much of each other as they needed to at other times during the day; the forty-two game and the telephone time were times they reserved strictly to themselves to be alone and cherish something of their sexual and personal privacy, I suppose.

The forty-two game was fascinating to me when I was a child, though I did not understand it, of course. (I was equally baffled by the doings of the Thursday Bridge Club when they met at our house, but I always got to lick the dasher from the apricot ice cream and that made it all worthwhile—that and the fascination of watching my mother's friends smoke and hearing them call each other "girl" when they were all well into middle age.) The forty-two game had to be played with those special cards; and they even played at a special table, more solid and sturdy than a mere card table, which one of the men had made. The furnishings of the Johnson Coal Company office were sparse, mainly consisting, after the chairs and tables, of a great roll-top desk; it was fascinating to me because it reminded me so much of an organ console, and I loved the organ music in church. I always pretended to be playing it on the back of the pew in front of me during all the hymns, even squirming about on the seat as though to reach the pedals, until Mamma looked at me to stop. The Heatrola in the coal company office was firmly installed on a metal plate and had two or three spittoons around its base for the men to use when they were chewing tobacco (my father never would wear his teeth when he did because he said they were clean and he did not want to get them dirty); they also served a purpose if the men just wanted to spit on general principles, to accentuate and make forceful their remarks, whether on life and morals in Woodville, the nation, or the world, or else when having one of the arguments about the game they all seemed to thrive on. O, there was an occasional cigarette smoker in the crowd (*they* never seemed to spit), but mostly the men chewed tobacco and smoked cigars. The atmosphere in the room was accordingly thick and heavy. My father usually favored the latter indulgence, and he had a wonderful cigar holder he had bought at the dime store and then whittled on with his pocket knife until it exactly fit the "Flor de Melba" brand of cigar he smoked. He would not have taken money for it. Indeed, once when he was driving his pick-up truck down Main Street in Memphis, he flicked his ashes outside the door and found, to his dismay, that the cigar holder had slipped out of his hand into the street. He just stopped the truck cold, got out and picked up the holder, and returned to the driver's seat while traffic on Main Street waited.

The game of forty-two seemed to revolve around bidding to

declare what denomination of cards would be trumps and then playing out the hand to see who could take the most tricks. Whichever side got its score up to 200 first won that particular game. At first it frightened me to hear these grown men get so excited about a mere game. Indeed, anyone who did not know them might have assumed that they were on the verge of a knock-down drag-out fight. I realize now, of course, that that was part of the fun. When they called each other damned fools or something else equally abusive (nothing ever obscene, though), they were signaling to each other—and perhaps to the outside world if it ever cared to listen—that they belonged to each other, loved each other, that each one had a place in the community and at that table. They had all known each other since boyhood, and there was therefore nothing new for them to learn about themselves; they could call each other names with impunity.

"Boosters" was what Daddy called those sideliners who never really did anything themselves but were always on hand if there was any excitement—at no expense to them of course, either in money or commitment—and especially if anything was being given away; for them the forty-two game and elections were made to order. Occasionally one of the boosters would get the sorehead and pout and pretend that his feelings had been hurt, but the regulars would have nothing of that. It was as though they were all saying, "If you can't stand the heat, stay out of the kitchen," and them that dished it out also had to be able to take it. They never really became offended by one another. O, occasionally, when one of them had been teased pretty hard, he might stay home for a night or two, but he would always come back. No one ever left the forty-two game except through death, for it was too important a part of their lives and the life of the community itself—what we would call an institution in that it gave dimension, depth, and meaning to their lives. But it would never have occurred to those men to put such things into words. That would have been half-way to destroy the hold and the power of the institution, to take some of the magic out of it by becoming self-conscious about it. Such things never, never ought to be put into words. When I was growing up, I used to get tired of hanging around the forty-two game, waiting for my father to get through for the evening and take me home, and I suppose it never occurred to me that he might be deriving as much pleasure from the forty-two game as I did from the picture show. But I eventually realized it, I think. I remember one night, when I was particularly tired of waiting for the game to be over, I jumped up and down and fidgeted around so much that afterwards Daddy threatened to wear me out if I ever behaved so again. I remember thinking: he is *enjoying* this game; it is his *pleasure*, and I have been wrong to interfere with it. I had never before realized that it meant so much to him. I had thought it was mainly a sparring match of sorts, with the men glowering at each other over their cards, thumping them down on the table to emphasize the determination behind each play, and raising their voices to call each other to order or make their displeasure known.

As the years went by and the older members gradually died off, Daddy said they already had a couple of tables of players in Heaven. The Johnson brothers, whose office they had played in all those years, died too, but the game continued. The surviving members of the group found a disused office over the Farmers and Merchants Bank and promptly rented that—complete with its own toilet so that they would no longer have to sneak out into the alley—for a nominal sum. The games went on from there. The Washington Avenue Forty-two Club went on, too, but its ranks were thinning as well. The young people around town seemed not to be interested in going on with or even learning the forty-two game. Was bridge such a powerful satisfaction, was it more demanding, was it more stylish, more chic? I suspect it was the latter. Forty-two smacked of the old ways, the old people—people who never allowed "spot" cards, "sin" cards in the house, people who looked on bridge and poker as certain highways to Hell. The younger generation was emancipated, already dreaming of putting Woodville far behind them some day for the glittering allurements of Memphis or some other big city.

After more of its players had died, the forty-two game was carried on at Mr. Jim Wilson's house, every night as usual. Mr. Jim was a widower and lived alone; therefore, no wife needed to be consulted in the matter. His health was not good, and I think his children were pleased to have him engage in some harmless recreation that would not take him away from home, for none of them ever objected to the nightly games. Every night, as regular as clockwork, Daddy would get up from the supper table and, without saying much more than a passing word to Mamma or me, he would go out and get in his truck and drive down to pick up Mr. Ed Hill, who, along with Mr. Jim Wilson and one or two others, made up the regular foursome. Occasionally, in bidding each other good night, they would say merely, "See you tomorrow night," or something like that. But as a rule, their social intercourse was minimal: the game was the thing, every night, and, it was understood, without the use of any social formulas. Their getting together for the nightly sessions that were part game and part ritual, certainly something of a ceremony, was a perpetual contract among them all that did not need to be spelled out. The old order at work? The old order at play? The old order simply in being? Whatever the game meant to them, and perhaps to the world outside, the need to explain any of it would never have occurred to them anymore than they would have ever felt compelled to explain their views on faith and morals, their attitudes toward life itself. The game extended and ultimately defined their personalities; it locked them into lives other than their own and fixed them irretrievably into a community of thought and action. It was their field for play but also a further means of grounding them in their society: they knew who they were, they knew where they were, and they certainly knew what they were doing. Their field of operation might have been narrow, just as Woodville itself was a small town in the rural South. But it was as real as could be for all that, and that was all that mattered.

As it turned out, Daddy was there at the last forty-two game that was ever played in Woodville, the night before Mr. Jim Wilson got sick with what turned out to be his last illness, though none of them knew it at the time. The next day he was taken to the hospital in Memphis, and he died about a week later. With his death they no longer had a whole table for forty-two, and no place remained for them to play with any regularity. I was away at college at the time, but Mamma told me all about it when I came home for vacation. She said Daddy was awfully lonesome then at night. They tried watching television together, but he could not get interested in anything that far away from Woodville. Too, they had little left to say to each other after so many years of marriage. Mamma tried to get Daddy to learn canasta, which was just coming in, but he said he had never held a "spot" card in his hand (remember his stern Methodist upbringing) and that he was not interested in playing a game with a lot of silly old women who really only wanted somebody new to talk to about their grandchildren. It was no fun for him; he knew it and she knew it. She said that most evenings he would sit in the living room with a coal scuttle beside him and a newspaper on the rug so he could spit when he felt like it. Then he would try to get interested in the evening paper, television, or anything else, but really he did not know what to do with himself. She said she was glad that he had not known that that night at Mr. Jim's would be his last one there or that he had just taken part in the last forty-two game that would ever be played in town.

✖ *A Christmas Visit*

I THINK OF *KING LEAR* and the color white—the color of age and winter, the color of despair. I sit in the waiting room after the receptionist has telephoned the "senile ward" that my patient has visitors, and I watch them drift by, the men in rumpled work clothes, the women in untidy cotton house dresses. More often than not, they are without their teeth, their chins and noses sometimes almost meeting, looking something like caricatures of their former selves, back when they were well, back when they were young. Their eyes often have a faraway look in them, sometimes bleared, as though they are trying to look beyond me, to see through me, into the future or, more probably, the past. The blues and the browns of the irises are faded now and the sparkle gone. Indeed, their eyes are almost lusterless, even opaque, sometimes even downright milky, especially when they seem to have lost all interest in looking outward and concentrate only on whatever vision can be discovered within. These are the ones whose worlds now are very private indeed.

They make little noise; they are well cared for, and they are clean. I can see that right off. ("O, there is a world of difference in things over there these days from what they used to be! Then they were just given food and a place to sleep. It's not an 'asylum' anymore, but a real hospital where people go—nobody is 'put' there these days— to get well and then come back home.") It is true that a meekness surrounds the ones there now—nothing really erratic or peculiar and certainly nothing violent or dangerous. ("Why, they don't have to use any kind of restraints on them now: the new drugs have made all the difference in the world! You won't see a thing to upset you over there—no more than you would out at the regular hospital here at home. It's just real nice over there: everybody ought to go over and see for himself.") These patients, the ones there now, are soft-spoken, sometimes even silent, but when they do turn their gaze toward me, I often notice something wistful about them, as though they are looking for something or someone but are afraid to ask for fear of being denied or rebuffed. What are they looking for; whom do they seek?

Is it some son or daughter out of the present, some friend or relative out of the past? Occasionally, one of them will stop and ask me whether I have come to see him; perhaps I will go along with him and say I have, which seems to satisfy him, for the moment, and he wanders off again. Or else he will stop and ask me when I last saw his family and when are they going to come and get him and take him home. I reply that I do not know but that I imagine it will be soon. What else can I say? Not the truth, certainly—that no one these days can handle such cases at home, that no one has the space or the servants to take care of them there, that no one has the time, for these days, life is definitely for the living—preferably the young. The dead must bury the dead, but I cannot tell them that. It is all I can do to tell myself that and make myself believe it.

There is a stir out front as new patients arrive: it is that time of day, the afternoon. A white man and a Negro woman are escorted in by a couple of deputy sheriffs, one of whom is a woman, and I wonder idly whether a troubled mind is still a crime. These two are not oldsters and therefore must be classified not as "senile" but as "insane." Did the deputies have to go out and "catch" this pair, maybe even arrest them and tell them to come along peaceably? The Negro woman, particularly, with her hair in wild disorder, looks agitated, and the woman deputy asks her to sit on a bench separate from the white man, who looks merely silent and subdued. Does that mean that racial segregation is preserved even into and beyond mental darkness, that there is no end to it anywhere, even in the grave? Or are they afraid that the woman will become violent at any minute and attack the man or someone else?

Again, the soft voices rise as the old people duck their heads in bashfulness and talk among themselves or to the nurses and their visitors if they have any. I look down at the legs of the women and they are often without stockings; all of a sudden, I think of all the naked legs outside the Nazi gas chambers, stacked row on row, the bodies of the victims arranged in orderly piles for *Life* magazine. What do they talk about? They hardly ever talk loud enough for me to hear. Is it just the minutiae of their daily lives, what they had for breakfast, what they want for supper, or are there complaints, misgivings, forlorn hopes, idle tears? Perhaps they discuss all of these. Now and then one of them will announce, as though no one else in the world cares (and who does?), "I've got to go to the bathroom," and then will wander off.

I notice the other visitors, too. They seem, on the whole, much like me, but we are reluctant to enter into conversation with one another. Indeed, we even avoid one another's eyes, as though sharing some secret shame. (A common sorrow, pure and simple, would bring us together.)

Finally, my patient comes, shuffling down the hall, holding onto a nurse's arm, taking the dance-like steps of the elderly arthritic, quick and short, as though anything else would be overly ambitious. As always, she is dressed in a clean print dress, her white hair beautifully combed and brushed. She is surprised all over again to see me, as though I am the last person in the world she had expected to see. Perhaps it is better than in the old days, when she first was a patient here, the times when she used to hug me and cry and beg to go home. She never talks about home now except to ask about various relatives and friends. Sometimes I have to tell her they are dead; at other times, I have to acknowledge that they just have not written.

She gets the home town newspaper, and I write to her once a week. So she knows all the news there is of a general nature. But she forgets: nothing stays long with her now, not even her surroundings. That is not to say of course that she does not know where she is, but where she lives is immaterial now; one place is as good as another. She has made a few friends among the nursing staff and with the other patients, but on the whole she holds herself aloof from them, perhaps seeing them as potential invaders of her private world. The old smile, somewhat puzzled now, is still there at times, and she still has the most gracious manners in the world—the courtesy that was grace itself and the tact that was famous. But all of this is somewhat perfunctory now, worn like a mask which has been on so long that there is no face behind it—automatic, ritualistic, dead.

The eyes are still blue. ("Blue is my color," she always said, just as she assumed an almost proprietary interest in arithmetic and algebra: "Mathematics was always my long suit.") But the vitality is gone from them: more and more, they seem to exist in repose—indifferent, uncaring, if not absolutely turned inward. They no longer are seeking, I feel; they no longer are waiting for anybody, anything. There is no outright retreat into the past, but a wall of impassivity seems to surround her, almost like a shelter, an impenetrable bulwark. Her peace with the world—at least with the present—seems made. O, there are flashes of the old wit from time to time. (She: "I never heard such cursing as there is over here, from the other patients." I: "Well, you haven't heard any words that you didn't know, have you?" She: "No, but some of the combinations have been unusual.") But more and more nothing is in evidence except a quiet politeness and a docility, a willingness to be noticed by anybody at all, but no great craving for attention. Because she is growing deaf, her voice, always kind and soft before, has begun to sound harsh and strident. Thus she may seem unhappy or petulant when really she is neither.

She shows me a little package of Christmas goodies some church group has brought her, along with all the other patients in her ward; it contains a wash rag and a bar of soap, a small box of talcum powder, and a little container of chocolate-covered cherries. She used to love those, and she could eat them now even with no teeth (perhaps that is why they were chosen), but she is indifferent about all the gifts, caring only enough to show them to me. I think: my mother is the object of charity, of philanthropy, however well meant; and I find that almost unbearable. Who would ever have thought it would come to this? But then what are the alternatives? There are none and I know it, for I have been through all that before.

I sit there a little while longer, with the poinsettia and some new print dresses I have brought her for Christmas. (My aunt: "They never seem to put the dresses on her that we bring; they're all just some sort of community property, I guess." I: "Well, they do the best they can, all things considered. She's certainly receiving better care than we could provide for her at home.") After a while, I get up and go into the Canteen and get some Coca-Colas for us both and also stop to ask there whether she still has money on deposit to use when she wants a snack. (She hardly ever does.) Soon the time arrives for me to go. And I have run out of anything else to say. What else can the two of us talk about anyway? More and more she has withdrawn into her own world, the world of the institution. She is not unhappy, nor is she really happy. She simply is. She no longer cries when I get up to go. I say, "I'll see you soon," and she says, "Come back real soon now." But does either of us really mean it or believe it?

The nurse comes back for her now, and she kisses me goodbye with some tenderness but no real sorrow and begins her shuffle back down the corridor. All of a sudden I feel inexpressibly sad though, again, it no longer tears me all to pieces to go over there as it used to. This is not a knife-edged sorrow now, rather more like a puzzled, reflective sadness as I watch her disappearing back into her ward. And I find myself wondering whether *she* has given all to her daughters—or to her son. Some lines of poetry, too, unbidden and unsought, begin to revolve in my head:

> For I could tell you a story which is true;
> I know a lady with a terrible tongue,
> Blear eyes fallen from blue,
> All her perfections tarnished—yet it is not long
> Since she was lovelier than any of you.

Outside the winter sky looms cold and bleak. It may snow before night.

❧ *Epilogue: The Old Tales, the Old Times*

I STILL GO OUT TO MAPLE GROVE to see one of my aunts—Aunt Mary, Uncle Jim's widow. Really, little else remains to draw me there anymore, now that my father and all but one of his brothers are dead. Still, I want to see Aunt Mary, and I want to hear her talk over old times at Maple Grove, when Daddy and Uncle Jim and the three other Drake boys were growing up out there.

I suppose now that nostalgia has become a rather fashionable emotion and the pursuit of the past something of a modish occupation I might be considered one who has simply fallen in with the spirit of the times. But I think not. The past is not something I took up just yesterday as a kind of hobby, something to play around with, something to have fun with. In many ways, I feel that because I was born into the past it has always been more real to me than the present. As the only child of older parents, I felt from the very beginning the claims that the past was making on me—and not always happily either.

When I was growing up, every Sunday afternoon of the world we would drive out to Maple Grove to see Pa Drake who lived with Uncle Jim and Aunt Mary. Daddy's three other brothers and their wives and sometimes their children (but not often because they were all nearly grown—much older than I) would usually be there too. Though they had grown up down the road on a little farm they still called "the home place," they seemed then to feel that Uncle Jim's house was their home—mainly, I suppose, because Pa lived there.

Pa was the only one of my grandparents I ever knew and I used to be afraid of him, partly because of his age, which made him seem

Pa Drake.

very formidable, but also because of his walrus mustache, I believe. (I was afraid of Santa Claus for the same reason; I wondered always *what* might be behind that beard.) With great reluctance I would let Pa catch me between his knees as he sat in the old high-back rocker that was his and draw me to him in a tight embrace and plant a moist, hairy kiss on my cheek. He smelled like an old man, too—not necessarily unpleasant but sweetish, somewhat overripe, and always redolent of tobacco from the corn-cob pipe he smoked

Pa seemed the most ancient man alive to me. He was almost ninety, but he had very few gray hairs: his hair was still that light sandy color that so many of my father's family were endowed with. And, because he had broken his hip years before, he could not get around very well. The main thing, though, that for me signalized his antiquity was that he was a Confederate veteran: he was a Virginian and had fought at Spottsylvania Courthouse and been at Appomattox when General Lee surrendered to Grant. I could not imagine how anybody could be old enough to have seen and experienced so much and still be alive to tell the tale.

Pa talked little about the war within my hearing. (We do have his wartime recollections, which he was persuaded to set down in his later years.) The fact of Pa's existence seemed somehow wonderful and strange to me: he had seen and done all that, and there he was still alive in the present, he whose eyes had looked at General Lee riding down the road on Traveler, he who had migrated to West Tennessee after the war, he who had outlived his wife and two daughters—but not his sons. He was a veritable sign and symbol of the past incarnate.

I remember, too, his addressing my father by his Christian name, which was the same as my own, and referring to me as "this boy." I was somewhat discomfited, for I realized that, though he was my grandfather and thus superior to me by all the rules of courtesy and manners, he was also superior to my father, whom I had never thought of as having to give in to anybody. If I was "this boy" to him, my father was also, and it was somehow disturbing to think of my father as being someone's son—just as I was myself—and having to say "yes, sir" and "no, sir," too.

The past could be quite humbling, I was beginning to find. Yes, I was taught to respect Pa, as I had been taught to respect Mamma and Daddy, but his claim appeared to be even stronger than theirs and they had to respect him, too. He was not only a father and grandfather but a Confederate veteran also, and, though I could not have put it into words at the time, I felt that he was in history, spoke out of history, and, perhaps to some extent, *was* history. That demanded respect because it was "the record" (as my Uncle John always called the photographs he took or whatever he was putting in his diary); you could not argue with "the record." It was there, remote but not detached, and indisputable, once the record was straight. Some sense of this feeling, this attitude I think I always had, and it was strengthened when I confronted its living embodiment in Pa. Of course, as I have said, I could not have put all this into words when I was growing up.

To tell the truth, I often thought the past was one great big bore. Every Sunday afternoon, we would all go out to Uncle Jim and Aunt Mary's, and the Drakes would sit there and tell the same old family tales over and over again until I thought I would die of boredom. Even after Pa's death we continued to go there; the star attraction might have finished his turn, but it was as though he were still present, dominating them in spirit, binding them forever to Maple Grove and the home place. I was puzzled by it all, to say nothing of being bored by it. They would sit there, in Aunt Mary's living room, some of them—particularly, my father—smoking cigars and rocking away in the old rocking chairs. They would egg each other on to tell the same old tales again and again about the things that had happened when they were growing up at the home place, about what went on at the Maple Grove Methodist Church, and also at the schoolhouse. The exchanges went on and on far into the afternoon. (I think Aunt Mary sympathized with the way I felt because, if we stayed long enough, she might even take me out to the kitchen and fix me a country ham sandwich.) The Drakes just sat there, relaxed and at ease, as though they had all the time in the world (which I now know they did—where else were they going?). They would nudge one another and say, "Now tell the one about the time. . . ." Sometimes that would be all that was necessary to set them all giggling, then arguing with each other about who had the straight of it.

I would fidget and get up and wander around the house and re-read all my cousin Laura's *Bobbsey Twins* books for the umpteenth time (or anything else that was lying around loose) and wonder when on earth they would ever get through telling their tales so that we could go home; I did not want to miss Jack Benny and Charley McCarthy on the radio. Sometimes, too, they would all be wiping their eyes when they had told a tale involving Grandma or the sisters, who were all dead. I thought that was funny, even silly: why did they tell a tale in the first place if they knew it was going to make everyone sad? Like a bunch of old women, I thought, having what they called a "good cry" over some of those idiotic radio soap operas, where everybody was having trouble. Why did they tell the same tales over and over again anyway when they all knew them by heart? As they sat there alternately talking and listening, they constituted almost a symphony orchestra: each one would sound his special motifs or passages (tell his special stories), then lapse into silence so that some other instrument (talker) could be heard. Even though I could not then understand it, I could sense that they were all part of some sort of complex orchestration, some communal recreation and celebration that meant a great deal to them but somehow eluded me. As I said, I found it all hard to understand, and I thought it was all a great bore.

All the talk centered around the old times and the home place. They never discussed anything relative to the modern day and age and not usually anything even as close by as Woodville, three miles away, where most of them lived, except for Uncle Jim and Uncle Wesley, who was at Barfield. Were they afraid of the present, the wider world, or were they just not interested in it? Their attitudes used to worry me a good deal. I could tell that they all derived some sort of sustenance from those Sunday afternoon sessions, that somehow they felt exalted and strengthened by what they had been participating in, both as individuals and as a group. Strange, I thought, that my aunts—their wives—should so willingly go along with it all. Did they not have tales they wanted to tell also? Or did they feel tongue-tied and dumb in the presence of so much memory, so much warmth?

These were all questions that I could not have put into words then, but they hovered unformulated in the back of my mind all those years while I was growing up. We would drive out to Uncle Jim's, passing the lane that turned off to the home place, and Daddy would never say much then; perhaps the actual home place—then rented out—held too many sad memories. At any rate, its time was over and done with. But when we and the other uncles and aunts arrived at Uncle Jim's, the atmosphere would brighten and spirits would pick up because, I could tell, the past was no longer dead for them and they could re-create it by their collective wizardry right there in Aunt Mary's living room. They *had* it then—unlike the old home place—and could relive it all at will. They enjoyed it so much, even when it was sad, which, as I said, used to puzzle me exceedingly.

I never could get any satisfactory explanation about it from Daddy, though. I would ask him why they all enjoyed telling all the old tales they had heard a million times over and over again, and he would just say that I would understand when I was older, a familiar adult retort that I always found infuriating. When I asked why they enjoyed telling even the sad stories, he would say merely that I had never lost anyone I loved, that I had no brothers and sisters, and that therefore I could not understand. It all seemed so unfair: on the one hand, I would have to wait until I was older to understand some part of those mysteries, and, on the other, participation in some of them would apparently forever be denied me simply because I was an only child who had never lost someone dear to him—no fault of my own.

The blood tie was sacred to Daddy, as was the home tie. He could never understand how anybody could fall out with his relatives, anymore than he could see how one could "get above his raising" and, in one way or another, renounce his home by going off to live in Memphis, much less Chicago or anywhere else up north. Such action was almost a sin against the Holy Ghost, to his way of thinking, for home and blood were the verities which defined who you were and where you were; to deny them was, in a sense, to deny the Spirit of Truth itself. Certainly, it was to deny one's own identity, which was a kind of spiritual suicide.

Exactly when I began to realize what the old times and the old tales meant to the Drakes I cannot say. Certainly, I do not recall that there was any blazing moment of revelation to enlighten me. I suppose simply that something like the truth of the matter did come with age, especially as the family began to die off. For many years, only Pa was dead and was therefore, more than ever, a focus for the Drakes' family piety, his former abode their spiritual home place. I remember how startled I was when at Pa's death, when I was nearly eight, my father caught me to him, in tears, and burst out: "You don't know what it's like to be nobody's child any more." I was disturbed and frightened to see, paradoxically, something of the child in my own father. Also I remembered my earlier feeling of surprise when I first realized my own father had a father too; I wondered whether he was not then feeling very much a child, an orphan and alone. He was basically unsentimental and could be quite businesslike even where death was concerned. I overheard him asking my mother how much she reckoned a "decent" coffin for Pa would cost. I felt scandalized because it sounded to me as though they were not going to do "the right thing" by my grandfather.

To see Daddy so obviously grieved for the loss of a parent was especially disturbing to me in that I knew that, because he and Mamma had both been middle-aged when I was born, I would lose them comparatively early. Thus death, loss, and sorrow became

The Drake family marker. Photo by Michael O'Brien.

early companions, even familiars for me as old people, old times, the home place, and the past were all early parts of my consciousness. I suppose I have had, all my life, to make a special effort to avoid getting old before my time. To this day, I am still more at ease with the old than I am with the middle-aged who are my contemporaries. I believe I know what they think, what they want, what they fear, and I believe I have learned something of what they know. The experience often is humbling, as I said earlier.

As the brothers died off (Uncle Jim was the first), the remaining ones grew even closer, and their Sunday afternoon sessions—still at Aunt Mary's—grew, if anything, more intense; they became more dramatically realized, more deeply felt. Paradoxically, the group laughed at the old tales even louder. Were they just whistling in the dark, or was it something deeper? Gradually then (because I was gone a lot, away from home at college, but also because I was much older) I began to realize something of what the Drakes had in their past, in the old tales, the old times. Even now after all these years it is difficult to describe exactly what I began to see they cherished, but I think it was some sort of consciousness on their part that the most valuable thing they had been given in their lives was the love and affection of their family: it defined the Drakes in time and place, and it stabilized them there. From it they knew who they were and where they were (assets singularly lacking to many people today, it seemed to me). So why not continually commemorate and celebrate (as they did in their tales) this great gift they had been given? The old tales were not being told therefore because they were new but because they were good. Though they were, in a sense, a private thing, what better way was there to share the great gift the Drakes had been given than by passing on the tales, through their gifted performances (Daddy and the others were splendid raconteurs) to others outside the family circle?

So even though the old times were occasionally sad, in memory they became consistently joyful because they were part of the Drakes' continual celebration of the great love which permeated and bound together the family circle. The real home place, down the road from Uncle Jim's, might stand as a solitary reminder that the dead were dead and the past was past, but in their tales it was ever transmuted into something very much alive, born again to give continual joy both to themselves and to others. Yes, there was sadness there; one made no mistake about that. But seen from a distance, as in their tales, the sadness, the losses, the dead all became part of the great seamless garment of the Drakes' love. Paradoxically, the dead still lived, and the past was ever present. This was the final wonder, perhaps the miracle of their tales, but only gradually did I realize it. Gradually, too, did I realize that, in learning something of the Drake past, I was learning something about myself, too: who I was, where I was, right there in the present.

They are all gone now, all except Uncle Buford, who was the youngest. And when I come home now on vacation, we have a great time retelling, just the two of us, the old Drake tales, and I know them almost as well as he does now, every verse in every hymn, you might say. I feel, too, that from now on I can freely enter into that wonderful world the Drakes used to re-create every Sunday afternoon out at Uncle Jim's at Maple Grove. But I had to earn that right by growing older and by keeping faith with the Drakes and trusting that their world did indeed have value even when I was too young to appreciate it. I know now, I believe, what it was all about, and it has become ineffably precious to me, a part of my very self. I still go out to Aunt Mary's. She is bedridden but still a great talker. And she and I rehearse the old Drake stories for a whole afternoon. Perhaps at her house, even more than at Uncle Buford's in Woodville, it all comes alive again; after all, I am nearer the source there—nearer to Maple Grove in the old days, the home place, the old times. And there are Pa Drake and all the family, the five brothers especially, back together again, all under one roof, as Uncle John used to say, larger than life, more real than ever now, and fixed forever in eternity, in all the talking, all the tales, all the love.

London—Venice—Florence—Knoxville
1975–1980